Confederate States of America,

Camp Magruder Augt 25th 1861

Dear Sister I write you a few
lines to inform you that we are
tolorably well at the present and
hope that you all are enjoying the

Confederate
Letters
and
Diaries
1861-1865

same health. We are now
neamped at Sidney Church about
three miles from Richmond I
like very well myself but Billy
is very much dissatisfied he is
getting home sick. We will stay
there we are now for two or three
months I hope, if not longer.
We have got our horces & Canon togeth
now, Capt Guys Company left this
morning for the western part of
Virginia They have been in service
for three months We drill five times
a day regualy Our Company has
determined on having Flying Artillery
hope that I will get a Corporals place.
If I do I will get a horse to ride
All Artillery Companies have 8
Corporals Capt Coleman has not
appointed any of the officers yet
We have 89 m
as taken sick with

Cover Art Concept by Walbrook D. Swank, Colonel, USAF, Ret.
Cover Photography by Tom Cogill

The acid-free paper used in this book meets the guidelines for permanence and durability of the Committee on Production Guidelines for Book Longevity of the Council of Library Resources.

First Printing, 1988
Second Printing, 1992

ISBN 0-942597-25-7

First Printing by
Papercraft Printing & Design Company, Inc., Charlottesville, Virginia, U.S.A.

Second Printing by
Burd Street Press, A Division of White Mane Publishing Co., Inc.
Shippensburg, Pennsylvania, U.S.A.

For a complete list of available publications
please write
Burd Street Press
Division of White Mane Publishing Company, Inc.
P.O. Box 152
Shippensburg, PA 17257

This book is dedicated to the memory of

*Private Hector Davis
Crenshaw's Artillery Battery (Va.)

†Private John Thomas Harrell
Co. K., 24th Virginia Cavalry

and

†Private Soloman Stewart
Co. F., 15th Virginia Cavalry

*the author's great uncle

†maternal and paternal grandfathers of the author's wife

About the Author

During his career in the United States Air Force, the author received numerous awards for distinguished service and at one time served a short tour of duty as a member of a Task Force in the Office of the Personnel Advisor to the President, The White House. Colonel Swank is a native of Harrisonburg, Va., and has had a long time interest in our Southern heritage and history. His grandfather, Thomas S. Davis of Richmond, Va., was a member of the 10th Virginia Cavalry and a relative of President Jefferson Davis. This is the third of five works written by the author about the 1861-1865 North-South conflict. He has assembled here a number of fascinating wartime letters and diaries of Confederate soldiers. These bring into sharp focus the hardships they faced on the battlefields, in camp, in bivouac, on the march, or in prison and reflect their deep concern for the safety and welfare of their relatives and friends on the homefront. The turbulent times are brought strikingly alive by the words of these men at war. He holds a Business Administration degree, a Masters in American Military History, and membership in the Bonnie Blue Society which is based on his scholarly research and published literature. He is the recipient of the United Daughters of the Confederacy's Jefferson Davis Medal and the Cross of Military Service. Among other organizations, he is a member of the Military Order of the Stars and Bars, the Ohio State University Alumni Association, and three Virginia historical societies. He resides with his wife at "Walbrook," Frederick's Hall, Virginia.

Contents

CHAPTER I.
Wartime Letters of Soldiers From Dixie

Contents *continued*

CHAPTER II.
War Diaries of Men Who Wore the Gray

Illustrations

Acknowledgments

In the preparation of this work, containing wartime diaries and many fascinating letters of Confederate soldiers, I am indebted, and express my deep appreciation to these contributors, and others, who helped make this book possible. Kenneth M. Lancaster of Louisa, Virginia, for letters and material relating to his ancestors James M. Hart, Charles D. McCoy, William K. McCoy, and Charles T. Shelton. Miss Mary Ogg of Trevilians, Virginia, for providing the diary and letters of her grandfather William W. Downer. Mrs. Carter Cooke of Louisa, Virginia, who offered the papers pertaining to her husband's great, great uncle James T. Anderson, his cousins Jimmie L. Lewis and James C. Ogg, and friend Joseph F. Bibb. Mrs. Josephine H. Neal of Louisa, Virginia, for the letter of Nicholas Johnson, her great-uncle. William H. Kiblinger of Mineral, Virginia, for documents and letters of his grandfather William C. Kiblinger of Rockingham County, Virginia. King McLaurin of St. Petersburg, Florida, for letters of his great, great-grandfather Allen Edens of Marlboro County, South Carolina. Mrs. Lewis H. Ford of Columbus, Ohio, for information and pictures pertaining to Camp Chase Confederate Cemetery, Columbus, Ohio. Louis P. Chisholm, Jr. of Mineral, Virginia, for letters of his great-uncle James O. Chisholm of Hanover County, Virginia, through the courtesy of the Virginia Historical Society, Richmond, Virginia. Bertram S. Allen of Louisa, Virginia and Welford M. Sims of Raleigh, North Carolina, for the diary of their grandfather Benjamin H. Sims of Louisa County, Virginia. William L. Terrell of Dillwyn, Virginia, for the letter of his great-grandfather, George H. Winfrey of Buckingham County, Virginia.

Introduction

Paramount in the thoughts of Confederate soldiers while defending their country on the battlefields was the exchange of letters and messages with their families, relatives, and friends at home. The receipt of letters, packages, and messages from relatives and girlfriends on the homefront served to strengthen their morale and helped them sustain their will and spirit to face the continued hardship and privation they endured on the march, in bivouac, in camp, in battle,—or in prison.

For the great majority of "Johnny Rebs," it was their first opportunity to travel for an extended distance from their own farms or communities and meet and observe various types and classes of people. They were eager to hear about life at home, the gossip, status of the crops and farm animals, parties, and the goings-on in the family.

Family and friends, in turn, were subject to a floodtide of letters from "Rebs" who described in detail their experiences about life in camp with comments about the food—its poor quality or the lack of it, shortages of equipment, animals, and the materials of war. With great delight, they reported about captured Yankee spoils, including such items as whiskey, sugar, coffee, shoes, clothes, blankets, guns, sabres, money, horses, pens, ink, and stationery.

Perhaps the most philosophical and penetrating letters were those that brought out the inner depths of character of each soldier. These were the descriptions of battlefield horror, bloody combat, the baptism of fire, the whistling of minie balls, the piercing screeching of canister and grape, the roar of cannonfire, the screams of the wounded, and cries of dying comrades. The fear, tension, stress, excitement, and the thought of possible death that would separate them from their loved ones at home brought to a head the emotions that would mature a youngster and "separte the men from the boys."

There being much interest in the 1961-1865 period in our national life, the author, in his research, has collected a number of interesting, unique, and fascinating letters and diaries pertaining to Confederate soldiers and events surrounding their wartime experiences. Repetitious thoughts appear in most every soldier's letter. The men were deeply concerned about the safety and welfare of their wives, children, and family. They were worried about the problems their wives faced in maintaining their homes and farms and the financial burdens they bore. Some wives gave birth to children while their husbands were away and some died with little ones to be cared for. These brave women faced all these stressful events with great fortitude, patience, energy, and courage.

Many of these letters are unedited and appear as originally written. Words are omitted only when they cannt bo interpreted or are unreadable due to the deterioration of the manuscripts.

"It is a duty we owe to posterity to see that our children shall know the virtues, and rise worthy of their sires."

President Jefferson Davis

Chapter I.

Wartime
Letters
of
Soldiers
From
Dixie

Letters of James Malcolm Hart

Private,
Crenshaw's Artillery Battery (Virginia)
    Pegram's Battalion
    Hill's Army Corps
    Army of Northern Virginia

Correspondence of a Confederate Artilleryman

This correspondence begins with the letters of James Malcolm Hart who was reared with his sister at "Brookville," Louisa County, Virginia. "Brookville" was the old Overton home in sight of Frederick's Hall Station on the C & O Railroad. He journeyed down to Richmond and enlisted in the well-known Crenshaw Artillery Battery on March 14, 1862.

This artillery battery took part in the principal battles of 1862 and distinguished itself at both Gaines Mill and Fredericksburg. At the latter place on December 13, James Hart was wounded and Lt. James Ellett, the ranking officer of the Battery, was killed. He was out of the Army for about six months, but the muster rolls show he returned to the Battery for duty in June 1863.

Though offered the responsibility of an officer, he remained a Private throughout the war. It is said that he was indeed a brave soldier, and did what he was bidden to do, but for volunteer service, he never offered himself. He was deeply religious, and it is said that if the Battery rested ten minutes, he would be sure to hold a prayer meeting. His letters state that he served through the war and the day before Appomattox took to the bushes to avoid falling into the hands of the enemy.

Crenshaw's Battery
Camp Lee March 19th. 1862

My dear Mother,

I have borrowed this piece of paper to drop you a line to let you know that I am faring well. Beef, bakers bread, rice, coffee, sugar, salt are the articles dealt out to us. We have quite a select mess. Thirteen stay in the same tent. I have my carpetbag, but have not been able to get my trunk up from town yet, and I have no chance to go down. Only 4 are allowed to go away at a time. We slept in our tents last night for the first time, on the ground. I have not felt any symptoms of catching cold yet & I have strong hopes that my health and strength will very much improve. My Irish substitute that I employed coming down gave me the slip the next morning. I saw Fred Pendleton, he is still uncertain about his destination. If he fails in getting into a place in the Quartermasters department I expect he will join us. Mr. Nuckolls will throw this off for me at F. Hall. I begin to think that a great deal of useless sympathy is thrown away "on the poor soldiers".

With love to all. I must close.

Yours in haste,
J. M. Hart

Crenshaw's Battery
Camp Lee Apr. 10th. 1862

My dear Mother,

You are wondering what your poor son is doing this horrid weather which feels more like winter than spring. You are hoping that it may not come to my turn to stand guard while it is raining and blowing. Well! It rained and it blew and what is more I had to stand guard but a kind providence protected me and here I am in better health than many of my more robust companions. I happened to have my post at the stable which fronted to the south and as the rain and wind came from the north I was completely protected, and with the aid of a fire that we kindled up, we passed our time quite comfortably. I stood from 12 at night till six in the morning and when my time was up I had a strong notion of going back to my post fire when I found that my mess had such a poor one and that all exposed to the wind and rain.

I had a very agreeable surprise a day or two ago since in the arrival of a large tin bucket of nicknacks from Mrs. Alexander Garrett. A baked chicken, a jar of pickles, slices of beef tongue, biscuit, and sweet cakes and pies. The next day it rained so that it was with difficulty that we could cook anything and you may be sure that we highly appreciated the present. It is not likely that we will have any worse weather than this and as I stand this very well I think you ought to dismiss your fears on my account. Forty of our horses have arrived and twenty of our men detailed to attend to them, consequently the detail from our company our general guard will be much less. You may expect one of my comrades up in a day or two who can tell you all about me. A Mr. Johnston to whom I introduced Uncle James. I wish you to get Ned McCloud to make me a pair of high quarter shoes to march in. I cannot wear these that are furnished by the government. Mr. Johnston can bring them when he comes back. Please write to me sometimes.

Yours affectionately,
J. M. Hart

18

Crenshaw's Battery

My dear Aunt Elizabeth,

I have broken open my letter to Mother to slip in answer to yours. Your letter was handed me this evening by one of our lieutenants, all our letters directed to the care of Capt. Crenshaw are put in the Captain's box and are brought to us the next evening after they arrive. The weather is becoming mild and pleasant again. The box is probably in Richmond Va. and if sent to the care of Mr. Garrett will probably be sent up to me. It will be very acceptable especially the bacon, I was about to say, but I believe on further consideration that each and every article will be especially acceptable. I see the daily Richmond papers every day. And important telegraphic rumors reach us sometimes in advance of their publication. Immense numbers of soldiers are constantly passing through here to reinforce McGruder. Great things must turn up shortly. An artillery company came in here today. They passed Louisa C. House last Sunday they said. They were in the Battle of Bull Run, Stone Bridge and Leesburg, their losses had been very small. They are going to the Peninsular. I shall write to Mr. Gentry soon. He passes as Mother's overseer I understand. I have not seen Mr. Overton since I left Louisa. A letter from Polly informs me that he had not returned from Winchester. Will was in the battle but escaped unhurt. Mr. Quisenberry that is with us is a brother of Charlotte Brenaugh's husband. His wife was a Miss Smith from the lower end of Spottsylvania. Talking in the tent has made me forget what I had got. I have an occasional tickling in my throat which makes me cough without spitting anything. I suppose it is something like Uncle Bill's cough used to be. Oh! I was going to say that I had got my new overcoat. It is a large coarse affair & I find no difficulty in putting it on over my old one which I do when it is very cold. My health, strength and appetite are all vastly better now than anytime for two months previous. My companions make no bones of telling me that I have been playing singe cat in pretending to be delicate. Give my love to my friends at F. Hall and at Woodburn & to every member of the Brookville family.

Your affectionate nephew,
James M. Hart

Crenshaw's Battery
Camp Lee April 18th. 1862

My dear Uncle,

Mr. Thomason a member of our Company goes up tomorrow. I propose to send up by him my uniform overcoat for Mother to make some improvements in. I wish the cape taken off and the underside lined with oil cloth, and then button holes worked at even distances around the collar so that the cape can be taken off and turned over, so as to have the oil cloth either above or below. If the button holes are not all the same distance apart they will not hit right when the cape is turned. Mr. Thomason returns Tuesday & will bring back the coat with him. I had my hair cut short in Richmond two or three days ago, and since that I wash my head all over in cold water every morning. I am entirely free from cough and cold. My last box came directly thru. We have quite flush times now in nicknacks. The Johnston's brought down several boxes for different members of our mess. We lack nothing now but a few horses and our knapsacks to be fully equiped. I have no news that you wont see in the dispatch as soon as you get this. Since writing the above I slipped down to town to get my overcoat. I saw Miss Amanda West at Mr. Garretts. Three trains were expected from Fredericksburg, which has been given up to the enemy. A friend is standing guard for me now so I must hurry. Goodbye.

Yours in haste,
J. M. Hart

Crenshaw's Battery
Camp Lee April 30th. 1862

My dear Mother,

According to promise this is sent you to inform you that we have this day received marching orders to report at Guinea's Depot in Caroline as soon as we possibly can. So in a day or two we will be on our way thither. A kind providence has so followed me with blessings and it would be ungrateful in you or me not to hope for their continuance. I am dreadfully bothered about my trunk and its contents. Besides what Crenshaw gives us I shall not attempt to carry anything but some flannel shirts and drawers. My writing materials must be dreadfully crumpled in my knapsack. They may get wet. My inkstand is already empty. It was turned over accidently. I mention these things to let you know how many things conspire frequently to keep one from writing in camp. Of course you cant help being uneasy about me, but I do hope that you will learn to cast all your cares on him who careth for you. Above all cultivate a spirit of submission to God's will. Think how short and unsatisfactory are all earthly things, and beware how you cherish any idolatrous love for them. Remember how miserable Aunt Betsy Hart made herself about her children all the time they were safe and well. I shall endeavor to leave my trunk with Mr. A. Garrett who will contrive to get it to you the first opportunity. My health was never better than now and I shall take all the care of it that I can. I wrote to you a long letter a few days ago. You or some of the family must write to me as soon and as often as you can. With love to all I am as ever

Your afft son, J.M.H.

Crenshaw's Battery
Camp Gregg May 12th. 1862

My dear Mother,

Although it has not been long since I wrote to you, a leisure moment tempts me to drop you a line to let you know of my continued good health. We have twice been out into the field to meet the enemy, but both times no enemy came. Yesterday about three o'clock a messenger from the general brought orders to hold ourselves in readiness for action. Our horses were instantly hitched and the men at their posts. Thus we remained, only a portion of the men sleeping an hour or two at a time, till this morning at half past three we were ordered to march. At sunrise we arrived at what I expected would be a battlefield. The brass pieces of our battery were sent forward and the rifled piece and the Marmaduke Johnson battery were placed in ambush behind the crest of a hill which commanded an extensive view of the surrounding country. In our rear was a rolling well wooded country, and before lay the flats of the Rappahannock, extending out in the direction of Fredericksburg. We common soldiers could only catch an occasional glimpse of the level country, as we were forbidden to show ourselves above the top of the hill. I made sure we were going to have a battle as we had gone forth with express orders to attack the Yankees. If they failed to attack us. But it was soon reported by our scouts that the enemy had retired beyond the river, and consequently we were ordered back to our encampment without a fight. Four days ago a similar disappointment when we were ordered to Massaponax Church. But that time it was all in the daytime. Almost everyone in our encampment is now asleep, although it is three o'clock in the day. There will be no drill this evening. About 11 o'clock or 12 o'clock since we returned to camp, I have heard upwards of 40 guns in the direction of town. It is supposed that the Yankeys are shelling the woods on this side the river to disperse any of our men who may be there in ambush. Twice couriers have come in announcing the enemy advancing in large numbers but when we go to meet them in force they always retire. When I last wrote to you we were soon to practice target firing. We went out and shot at a mark about ten feet square at a distance of six or eight hundred yards. The mark was struck by 4 or 5 of the shot and shell. The shooting was pronounced very satisfactory by judges. Genl Gregg was present and sighted one of the guns himself. Our rifled pieces were not fired. Ammunition suited to our field pieces was too scarce to be thrown away in the air. We are near what is called the Summit Level. It is a ridge of land between the Rappahannock and Mattaponi Rivers, and the railroad has a steep grade going each way from here. They say that a car let loose here would run into Fredericksburg of themselves if not stopped. The woods here begin to be covered with leaves and at night to be filled with the whippoorwill's note. Give my love to everybody at home and write soon.

Your affectionate son,
James M. Hart

Crenshaw's Battery
Camp Shield May 21st. 1862

My dear Mother,

A gentleman from Wallers Tavern is here today and as there is much uncertainty about the mails I have thought best to send a letter across the country. We have moved our camp about 4 miles from the Summit. We are now encamped on a cloverfield belonging to a man named John F. Alsop. We are about 4 miles from Fredericksburg. There is a very small prospect of a fight ere now. We have no knowledge of our future movements. Much will depend on what is done in Richmond. The result is looked for with interest. We stand a very good chance I think, not to get into a fight at all. The gentleman who is here is a dentist, and he can give directions at Wallers Tavern to Uncle James where to find us. Robt Kinney told me that Uncle James talked of paying me a visit. If he could come and find it convenient to bring me anything to eat, I cannot think of anything more suitable for camp than eggs packed in meal. Wash the eggs and sift the meal, both meal and eggs are wanted. We are 22 miles from Wallers Tavern. I have the satisfaction of hearing from your neighborhood through Elias Hancock, who receives letters oftener than I do. I have been looking for F. Harris here for sometime. I heard that he was in Richmond waiting for his uniform to be made. We are somewhat expecting to be sent from here to Culpeper. If so we shall probably join Jackson to invade the North. A report has reached us that the Yankees have evacuated Fredericksburg. False report I expect. We occasionally hear of our men taking a few Yankees, and sometimes they take some of our men. But these things occasion no excitement here. We have a good many artillery companies encamped near here. They drill on the same field. I must bring my letter to a close as the R. may soon wish to start. Give my love to the girls at Woodburn, to F. Harris and other enquiring friends. I wish I could have been with you all. We see no ladies here. Be sure to write to me as often as you can. Direct your letter to Guinea's Depot Caroline Co. Care of Capt. Crenshaw. With love to all I remain

Your affectionate son,
James M. Hart

⁓

Crenshaw's Battery
Headquarters Crenshaw's Battery June 21st 1862
Dr. Friends House Opposite Dr. Gaines
Headquarters of Genl G. B. McClelland

My dear Mother,
I see that this morning's Enquirer has a short account of a fight which took place on our lines yesterday in which the celebrated Crenshaw Battery did some excellent shooting. You will naturally wish to know what part I took in the fight. I was suffering from a boil on my neck at the time but not wanting to miss the excitement of one action I went along with our gun (No. 6 Rifle Gun) till we found Lieut. Ellett & Johnston at a place which you will find on the map I drew in my last letter to you, "Masked Battery" under James Ellett". Our guns were placed in position and pointed at a Yankee Battery about 800 or a thousand yards distant, with orders to fire as soon as we saw the flash of the Yankee guns. We had to peep through our concealment of pines and leaves & tree tops to see our mark. The guns were loaded with shell, with their fuses cut so as to burst four seconds after leaving the muzzle of the gun. The wished for a moment at last arrived and one after another our four guns 2 rifles & 2 six

pounders, opened. Our guess at the distance was lucky and the firing would have done credit to veterans. Just in front of the Yankee battery our shells burst and the enemy did not think proper to reply. What was certainly done we had no means of finding out as the Yankee battery was masked, as well as our own, behind bushes which shed a few of their leaves at every fire. Owing to my boil rendering it painful for to move about much, I was detailed to hold the horses to the limber, and an abled bodied driver took my place at the gun. Long Tom and Big Bess (large rifle cannon under Capt. Dabney) in the meantime were paying their respects to larger and more distant batteries higher up the Chickahominy. The papers have published the result. A Yankee battery on a hill to our left had been annoying us for several days, having actually made three holes through the tobacco house in which my detachment was in the habit of lounging in the day and sleeping at night.

The first fire of Long Tom at this battery dismounted one of their guns and caused the cannoniers to retire. Our tobacco house (put down on the map I drew for you in my last letter) furnished such a good mark for the Yankees that our General (Gregg) made us pull it down. After the firing was over we hitched up our guns and returned to our former position. June 22. My boil is better today and I suffered less pain last night than any night since I had it. I expect the core to come out this evening when it will soon be well. I have a plaster on it of turpentine soap. This is the second boil I have had on my neck within the last two or three weeks. The Captain laughs at me and says my looks show that I live high. Today is Sunday but nothing of duty is abated on account of the day. At 9 o'clock a.m. we have an inspection. Each has to appear in line with his uniform and knapsack on. I was excused from putting on my knapsack. What do you reckon we had for dinner today? We had some beef soup and biscuit. Good enough for anybody. My messmates are

Lewis Nuckolds (wheelwright) Thaddeus Johnston (commisary sergeant) Joseph Johnston (quarter master sergeant) and several others like myself without any office. The advantages of this mess are many. Joe Johnston's office takes him to Richmond every day or two to buy corn and hay for the Co. & then we can get little parcels brought and carried, bread, crackers, sugar, coffee, tea, & are thus procured. Thaddeus Johnston carries our commissary stores and thus we can carry along things which otherwise would have to be left behind. Nuckolds tool chest carries many a little parcel, this paper, for instance. The Yankees are very quiet today. Long Tom shot at their balloon today. The balloon thought it best to descend. I cannot close this letter without mentioning some of the rumors that float through our camp. The most exciting to us is the one which anticipates the disbanding of our company on the following conditions, that each member shall choose to avail themselves of the conscript law. That part of the conscript law forbidding reenlisting men from changing their arms of service has deprived our co. of upwards of forty men; who expected to join in as soon as their term of service expired.

These places were kept for these men, till it was too late to fill them with others that would be acceptable. A certain Captain Alexander was a co. which was recruited to man a stationary battery which co. for the want of arms (cannon) has been placed in the infantry. Many members of this co. were anxious to be transferred to our company but the efforts made to effect the transfers have been unsuccessful. The generals concerned saying that they have more artillery already than they know what to do with. We have not men enough to man our guns now, and to lessen the number of guns would take away the commission of some of our officers. I understand that the Captain has offered to disband the company on conditions mentioned above. I got Mr. Nuckolds to read the above to see whether my cross writing is legible.

He says I ought not to have written the above as it might raise false hopes in your bosom. If I am not allowed to repeat the rumors of our camp I shall have little to write. And if a mere rumor is going to turn your head why you had better not hear things. You all must write soon and believe me most affectionately yours,

James M. Hart

Crenshaw's Battery
Madison Station
Monday Aug 31st 1863

My dear Uncle,

A man exempt from military duty paid me a visit yesterday to get the place of overseer on my farm. I referred him to you, so you may expect him in a few days down on the accommodation train. He is now living with Oliver Terrel. I was at Hartland the day you left. Mrs. Gentry and negros seem to have a very poor opinion of each other. I was glad to hear that you had employed Mr. Payne to attend to threshing the wheat I suppose the government has knocked the flour business in the head. We are entitled to keep seed and fifty bushels for family consumption. This much had better be ground wheat is worth 3 dollars, worth more in flour than in wheat (letter torn) their horses, and exposing themselves to the danger of being shot or frost bitten.

We draw some sugar each day. We have bacon and fresh beef issued to us alternately. I got some potatoes when I was at Hartland they are not bad. We are living very well. The nights are very cool, but the days are pleasant. The tenth part of my oats and hay have been delivered, and the clover hay at Smith's shop besides. This was admitted at 2000 pounds. Joe Johnston says he will pay me when he gets the money from his superior . . . .

※

Crenshaw's Battery
8 miles from Chancellorsville
Oct 5th 1863
Camp Germaniner Ford on the
Rapidan River

Dear Mrs I take the pleasure this morning to drop you a few lines I recived a letter from Mrs. Gentry last night and she informed me that she been treated very kinde by you and Mr. Claybrooks and I think it my douty to return same thanks to you both for your kinde treatment to her. I am more then oblige to you both for the good and kindness you have sharne hir and I dante onley thank you both bout if it so please our Almity Farther to spair me to return home saft again I will try and dou somethin in return for such good and kind treatment as she has received from you all I shal never forget you all for such kind treatment. Mrs. Hart anything that Mrs. Gentry can dou for you I want you to let hir no it an she will dou it I have written to hir to that affect donte you ab fread to give hir such jobs to attend as you my wish done to she will dou them and think it hir duty to dou so and she is willing to dou any thang for you that is in hir power to dou. Mrs. Hart tell Mr. Claybrooks to write to me. Wee have a hard time and it is at this time wee are fortifying this river from Rapid Dan Stashun to Frericksburg wee wark day and night some of our men went over the river the other night and captured 3 horses and one Yankey and killed one and wounded another last week we went over and got an hundred sheep and several cows we had to go over in night and we killed one Yanke that trip the pickets is very clost togeather well I must close my short letter as I am standing guard and it is time for releaf when you write directletter so. Wm. H. Gentry Company D 44 Va Regt 2 Bragade Johnson Division care of Capt L. T. Woodson Orange C.H. Tell Mr. Hart I shud wrote him but I dont kno whar to direct the letter may the grace of God be with you all both now and forever I am respectfully

Wm. H. Gentry

Crenshaw's Battery
November 30th 1863

Dear Mother,

I am not more than 20 miles from you; our position is on the line of railroad from Orange Court House to Fredsburg, not far from the Spottsylvania line, about 12 miles north from where Uncle James Hart used to live. Mr. Lumsden is here now to see his son, & will take this note to Twymans Store for me. I belong to the reserve and may not have to go into the fight at all. Our battery is in position and did some firing last evening and this morning. You no doubt can hear our guns. I hope your trust is in God and that you will be enabled to cast all your care on him who careth for you. I have a culvert on the R.road to retire to if necessary. We have 30 men in reserve. Mr. Lumsden is about to start, good bye, Your son, J. M. Hart

Crenshaw's Battery
December 1st 1863

I wrote you a note yesterday which you will get probably at the same time that you get this. I do not think proper to tell you anything about the disposition of our army. I write to let you know that I am one of thirty men who are held in reserve and that there is a strong probability that I may not be called into action, during the fight which is expected to take place very soon. The two armies are in sight of each other both apparently afraid to attack its adversary. We are confident of success in case they attack us. We had a very cold night last night, the soldiers who had to lay in the trenches no doubt suffered much. I cant tell you any news that you don't see in the papers. Mr. Richard Lumsden comes to see us every day.

Crenshaw's Battery

I am on the line of rail road leading from Fredericksburg to Orange Court House about five miles north from Mr. Lumsdens who lives about three miles from Tyman's Store. The firing that you heard yesterday was done by Ewell's troops whose entrenchments were charged three times by the Yankees who were repulsed three times with great slaughter. Our line of battle is ten or fifteen miles long and a partial fight might take place without our knowing anything about it till a day after it occurred. We (the reserves) stay several hundred yards in the rear of our battery in a bottom which the rail road crosses over on a rock culvert into which we can all creep when any firing in front frightens us into our holes. The Mr. Coleman from Nelson county is a grandson of Uncle Hawes and is a conscript in our battery. You will recollect him as the man who borrowed a horse to go over to Mr. DeJarnettes. He says he don't mean to go into the culvert because it might stigmatize him as a coward. We laugh at his scruples and expect to see a wonderful change wrought in him by the force of example the first time a Yankee shell comes in dangerous proximity. I will write to you every chance I get to send a letter till after the dreaded conflict is over. Praise God for his past and present mercies and trust to his goodness for the future. Cast all your care on him who careth for you. This may fall into the hands of the enemy so I must be cautious. Goodbye

(Written in pencil, undated, undirected, unsigned, but in the handwriting of J. M. Hart)

Crenshaw's Battery
December 4th 1863

My dear Mother,

I wrote you two letters from what I supposed was about to be a battlefield, one dated November 30 and the other Dec 1st. We were well entrenched and every way prepared for the enemy. We waited two whole days for the enemy to make the attack but except the charge made on Ewell's which was handsomely repulsed, they made none. The third day it was determined to attack the enemy but when the time came the enemy was gone. We are now at our old encampment near Mr. Ferdinand Jones' on Mr. Graham's land about two miles north of Orange C. House and about one mile from Eliason's Mill. If Uncle James should find time to come out to see me, he had better come to Mr. Jones' to spend the night as he would be very uncomfortable in camp at night. When I started on our last march I gave my money ($300) to Mr. Lewis Nuckols to take home with him, as he was with the wagons that were sent in that direction. Uncle James can get this money whenever he wants it. I sent my boots the same way but Mr. Nuckols forgot to leave them. It seems that the Yankees were afraid to attack us. It is reported that a certain portion of the Yankee Army volunteered to charge our position (Pegrams) but they saw how well fixed we were, they changed their minds. Two nights we expected a night attack. Everything was kept in readiness. Charges of canister were placed near the muzzles of our guns and one detachment kept on watch. Two hundred yards in front of our guns was a row of rifle pits for our sharpshooters, when these had been driven in behind our guns and brestworks, we were to let fly with our grapeand canister, no troops could have stood such a flood of death as we would have poured into their ranks. Many were the knapsacks, overcoats, canteens, oilcloths, blankets &c that we expected to find when the contest was over. I want two new undershirts as those I have are much the worse for wear especially about the wristbands and collar. We are anxious to hear from Braggs Army. The papers have reached us irregularly lately.

I hope it wont be long before we go into winter quarters. I know you all have a great deal to tell me when you write, but like myself when you are writing you forget, many things. Now what I want you to do is take a piece of paper the size of this and place it in the map where it will be convenient for each member of the family to write whatever they want, and when it is full seal it up and send it off. Be at least two or three days about it. Your last letter was full of news and interesting accordingly. I sent back my old clothes in the same box that contained my new clothes. The overcoat I sent I bought from Luck for $8. I thought that the cloth in it would be worth that much. When Uncle James gets his coat wet that coat will do to change. I wrote Dr. Quarles to forward the box for me from Gordonsville and that Uncle James would pay him the freight on it the first time that he saw him. Let me know whether the box has ever arrived and what was in it. How do you like my blue patches that I put on my breeches? I reckon that you all laughed at it but I think it was done very well for the first patching that I ever did. When my hogs are killed I want the tongues saved for me. How I do wish that I could be with you all to enjoy the brains, little bones-spareribs, &c. A good many families suffered the loss of all their years supply of meat whilst the Yanks were in Spottslvania. I was told that some had just killed and their hogs were taken down for them. Gadison Johnson a member of our mess had a brother, a tanner, whose tanyard happened to fall within the enemy's lines. He had everything that he possessed destroyed. The next meat you send me let it be fresh, fat and free from bones, and salted well. We can make lard of the fat for our bread. Some dried fruit would not go amiss. Indeed nothing comes amiss. Good apples sell readily for 25 cents a piece. Turnips the same. 1 head of cabbage $1.50 to $2.00 sorghum molasses of inferior quality $5.00 per quart & other things in proportion. Now get your paper & begin that letter described above.

J. M. H.

Crenshaw's Battery
Dec 16th 1863

My dear Mother,

We are now putting up winter quarters about a mile from Mechanicsville, and about 2 miles from Linsay's Turnout on the Va. Central R.R. We have to work on the stable every day beginning at 9 o'clock. We work on our own house at night and whenever not otherwise engaged. Having to march soon after Mr. Cash came to our last camp I had to sell some of the articles. I got $11.25 for the small ham and $3 per peck for the potatoes and the same for the meal. I dont wish anything more sent me until our winter quarters are done. We have barely time to cook and eat the simplest fare I got our commissary to carry all my small bags and apples. I am delighted with our molassses. Indeed we were not certain that it was molasses. I have not time to write more.

Crenshaw's Battery
Camp Taylor,
Jan 27th 1864

My dear Mother,

It is not day yet and I am up this early because it was my day to make up the fire in the morning. The cars made but poor headway the day I came up as it was night when I arrived at Hartland. The next day I took dinner at Prospect Hill and staid all night. Thursday I came to camp. No questions were asked me about my long stay. Friday was taken up in cleaning up the camp, to which drudgery we have given the name policing. Saturday I was on guard. Whilst I was standing at my post guarding our corn and other horse feed, a man named Desper who lives near Mr. Overton drove up in a one horse wagon with persimmon beer, tobacco, &c to sell. At his request I enrolled in our company his two nephews who he said wished to join us. They promise to report on or before the first of February. If they fulfill their promise and are mustered in I will be certainly entitled to a thirty days furlough and perhaps to sixty days. Genl Lee has offered thirty days for each new recruit, but there is a difference of opinion as to whether more than thirty days can be claimed by any one man. Major Pegram thinks I will get sixty days but other officers think differently. Sunday I went to church at Mechicsville, heard John Jones preach. In the evening he preached at our log chapel. Monday I went to see Mr. Desper to hurry up my recruits & took dinner at Mr. Overtons. Edloe Bacon was there recruiting his health. Mrs. Lucian Minor in there teaching. Polly is in Richmond. Yesterday (Tuesday) we had an inspection. I will write again before very long.

Yours in haste,
J. M. Hart

Dec 26 to Jan 24th 1864. (Absent 29 days)

Brookville Feb 2nd 1865

My dear Uncle Thomas:

The last letter we had from you was dated August last. Sad changes have taken place here within the last twelve months. On the last day of February my dear Aunt Elizabeth breathed her last, and on the 19th of June she was followed by my dearest of mothers. Grace was granted to both to leave life with great resignation in the hope of a blessed immortality. Let us all try to live so as to be prepared to meet them in a happier state of existence, where "the wicked cease from troubling and the weary are at rest". Aunt Sally has a Miss Hall staying with her to assist her in the discharge of her domestic duties. Aunt Sally & Uncle James are both in the enjoyment of their usual health. The servants also are as well as usual; some few among so many, being almost always on the sick list. My servants, at Hartland, whom I saw a few days since were all well. My health is usually good. Within the last six months I have gained twenty pounds in weight. We are anxious to hear from you. A letter directed to Petersburg Va., would reach me, but you had better write to Uncle James at Fredericks Hall. My uncle & aunt join me in love to you.

Yours affectionately,
James M. Hart

In December 1865 James M. Hart married Miss Mildred Dabney Farrar, a daughter of Col. Stephen and Susan P. Farrar of Louisa County, Virginia. During the next year he purchased a plantation and mill on the South Anna River where he settled and remained until he died in 1889. At this place he conducted a school for boys, having five of his own, and many throughout the neighborhood. He was buried at Hartland.

To: Mr. Thomas W. Claybrooke
    Bell's Station
    Madison County
    Tennessee
Care of: Mr. Thos Noel

Brookville July 1st 1866

My dear Uncle,

The interruption of the mails and my not knowing till lately how to direct a letter to you, are the principal reasons for my long silence. You have no doubt, heard from Uncle John that I survived a four years service in the late war and that my health was improved by the hardships of a soldiers life. I was wounded only once although I was very often exposed in time of battle. I have entirely recovered from my wound except that I limp a little sometimes in walking down hill. I belonged to an Artillery Company, and it give me great satisfaction to remember that my battery did good service and was often assigned to posts of honor, and never disappointed the expectations of our officers, but once, and then the ammunition (and not the men) was in fault. On the 7th day of last December I was married to a Miss Mildred D. Farrar daughter of Col Farrar an old gentlemen living about 15 miles south from F. Hall. I have been living on my farm near the Green Springs ever since Lee's surrender & teaching school there since last September.

The collapse of the Southern Confederacy left me without a cent of money and with no labor but hired labor. The consequence is, that I am very hard run and my neighbors' being in the same fix does not make it any better for me. The wheat this year is the greatest failure I ever knew. The most liberal estimate suppose that seed & home consumption will be barely supplied. Hence it is that nothing being sent out of the county no money has come in, certainly very little except in the way of a loan. When we want anything at a store sugar & coffee for instance we take a few pounds of butter or some chickens, eggs or bacon, lard &c and exchange them for the goods we need. I need not tell you this system of barter is extremely inconvenient, and occasions many a man to ride on horse back that otherwise would go on the car. Some few of the freedman are doing well and giving great satisfaction to their employers but as a general thing they are disposed to waste their time, and what is harder still to bear to be insolvent.

I have not a single one on my farm that formerly belonged to me. With the exception of one woman, my hired servants do well enough. But for this money received for teaching school I have no idea that I should be able to meet expenses. You will perceive from the dating of this letter that I am writing at Brookville. Uncle James and Aunt Sally are both well and send their best love to you. Fred Louis Harris rode over in his carry all this morning and requested me to send his love. Uncle James is now in the midst of his harvest and finds his wheat very bad but a considerable quantity of oats will be made and the corn looks promising. I received a letter not long since from Uncle John, from which I was pleased to hear that you had suffered but little by the war, as also how I would have to direct this letter. My post office is Trevillians Louisa Co. Va. I hope you will let me hear from you soon by letter, or what would be far better that you will pay us a visit and see for yourself how your relations are getting on in Va. I wish you to see how I conduct myself as a married man. If you could see how much comfort is added by the presence of a wife, you might be tempted to marry yourself. I am going to canvas this county as agent for the sale of a book (Dr. Dabney's Life of Stonewall Jackson). I hope by leading an open outdoor life to recover some of the strength lost during the last ten months confinement in the school room.

Your affectionate nephew,
James M. Hart

My dear Uncle — I arrived here last evening and was rejoiced to find a letter from you which put to flight all my sad suspicions that you had entirely put us out of your mind, in these days when friends seem disposed to give place to misfortune which crowds in where all others are glad to leave. During the war and since I have written again & again until the thoughts of wearying you worried me. As you say that you have received no letters from me, I need not hesitate to repeat some portions of my past history, which I had thought would interest you.—In the spring of 1862 I joined the Army and served with all the ups & downs of a private soldier till the day before Lee's surrender, when I took to the bushes to avoid capture by the enemy. On the 12th December 1862 I received a severe wound at the Battle of Fredericksburg by which I was disabled for seven months. I am still a little lame at times. On my return home I found as you have no doubt heard from other sources, that I was left alone in the world, a state so lamentable to be in, that I forthright paid my addresses to Miss Mildred Farror, (not Miss Sally who was a red head) a young lady with beautiful auburn hair. I was married the 7th December 1865. On the 31st August 1866 I was presented with a son and a daughter at the same birth. Their names are Mary Claybrooke & Malcolm Duncan. Two prettier children are not to be found in the whole country. Mary is very much like my mother, dark eyes, dark hair and beautiful features, she runs all about and is as playful and active as a kitten. Malcolm is more like Uncle Jim, blue eyes, fair skin, light hair (not red) he is much more of a baby than his sister and has the bump of caution well developed, so much so, indeed, that he cannot trust himself to walk alone.

On the 17th September 1866 I attended the sale of the landed estate of Abner N. Harris deceased. The mill and two hundred and thirty four acres with the dwelling house were put up at public auction & I became the purchaser at $26.25 per acre. I had tried farming with free labor on my farm in the Green Springs & found it a losing business & thought I would try milling where I could find full scope for the indulgence of my mechanical ingenuity. My dependence to pay for the place was to sell my Green Spring estate. I accordingly disposed of that to two men who paid me $850 towards the first payment & then flew the contract. I have now both estates on my hands and am deeply in debt. The executor has sued & will get a decree for a resale next April, unless I succeed in selling before that time, and meeting my engagements. Milling is not so profitable now as it used to be. People that used to send a barrel now send a bushel & others in proportion. What you say about going to the dogs in Tennessee is equally true of us here. When I compare our former wealth with our present poverty I am filled with amasement at the greatness of the change!—I will now tell you something of this neighborhood. Dr. and's (Chas Harris) place is occupied now by his sons & daughter. They gave $18 per acre!! The land was rich when you knew it compared with what it is now. Dr. Wm. Pendleton lives where he did when you were in Va. Indeed I do not now think of any changes of residence. Unless I may except Abner Harris a son of Hillary Harris of Powhatan Co. has married Nat Harris daughterand bought a piece of land from Uncle Jim & settled on it. His residence is between Locust Grove Spring & F. Hall Depot. I send you an example of wighting in cypher which you will readily understand, if you will notice that one letter is put for another & can be readily read by reference to the key, which you can make yourself if you only know which letter stands for A. Under the letter c in Uncle you will notice a mark from that you can make out your key. It might be any other letter as well.

42

B

Letters of Charles Daniel McCoy

Captain,
25th Virginia Infantry
    Early's Division
    Ewell's Army Corps
    Army of Northern Virginia

Charles Daniel McCoy was the son of William McCoy and Sally Ann Kemper McCoy of Charlottesville, Virginia.

Charles McCoy was a Captain in the 25th Virginia Infantry. He was captured at Spotsylvania Court House 12 May 1864 and imprisoned at Morris Island, South Carolina. He was a surviving member of "The Immortal Six Hundred" and died 11 September 1879. The "Immortal Six Hundred" were Confederate officers who were federal prisoners shipped to Morris Island in Charleston, South Carolina, Harbor. These prisoners shielded the Yankees on the Island from Ft. Sumter's guns across Charleston Harbor.

The prisoner's food was scarce and of the poorest imaginable quality. According to Captain J. O. Murray of the 7th Va. Cavalry, "It consisted of four hardtack army crackers, often rotten and green with mold, and one ounce of fat meat, issued to us at morning roll call; for dinner we received one-half pint of bean or rice soup, made as the caprice of the cook suggested; for supper, we were allowed all the wine we could inhale."

A diary left by Captain A.M. Bedford, 3rd Missouri Cavalry, said this about the food on September 11, 1864, "Rations for dinner, one-half pint of bean soup, two crackers (full of worms and bugs). A.J. Armstrong and myself had to pick out the worms before eating. Water full of wiggle-tails today."

Captain MacRae stated that, "Some of the prisoners, for the sake of the record, complained to Colonel Hallowell about the lack of meat and the wormy, buggy crackers. He replied that it was all right there was meat enough in the crackers, bugs and worms; and that, if he had his own way, he would be only too glad to feed us on greasy rags."

No toilet facilities were provided for the Confederates for more than thirty days after their arrival on Morris Island. On October 6, 1864, an order was issued to Colonel Hallowell instructing him to requisition enough lumber and supplies to construct proper toilet facilities for, "the rebel officers, prisoners of war in his charge." It needs no stretch of the imagination to visualize the deplorable sanitary conditions that must have existed in the two-acre compound *after more than a month's occupation by six hundred men. Despite efforts by the Federals to justify their actions of imprisoning Confederate officers in an exposed position, claiming that the Federal prisoners in Charleston were being similarly treated, there is not much evidence to support their statements. This is verified not only from the accounts of the Confederates who survived, but in the Official Records of the war published by the United States government in 1891. The exact number of those who survived has never been ascertained. W.B. Allen, First Lieutenant, 6th North Carolina Regiment, stated in the Confederate Veteran that "I have understood that one hundred and fifty out of six hundred died in three months."*

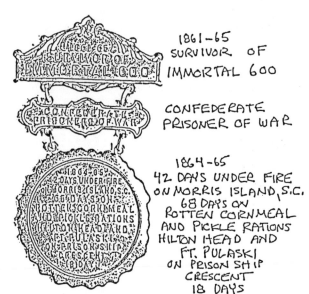

1861-65
SURVIVOR OF
IMMORTAL 600

CONFEDERATE
PRISONER OF WAR

1864-65
42 DAYS UNDER FIRE
ON MORRIS ISLAND, S.C.
68 DAYS ON
ROTTEN CORNMEAL
AND PICKLE RATIONS
HILTON HEAD AND
FT. PULASKI
ON PRISON SHIP
CRESCENT
18 DAYS

Medal of the "Immortal 600" (Obverse).

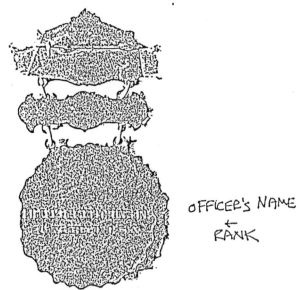

OFFICER'S NAME
← RANK

Medal of the "Immortal 600" (Reverse).

1861-65 Survivor of the "Immortal 600" Medal

46

On the field Dec. 14th. '62
Sunday evening

Dear Mother

We are in line of battle a few hundred yards from the enemy. You are all uneasy I know. Ken & I are safe. Ken was under fire yesterday tho' not engaged. Legh told me this, this morning. He saw Ken late yesterday evening. I was in a hot fight from 2 to 3 1/2 yesterday. We have repulsed the enemy at every point. I expected the fight to be renewed this morning but there having been only some skirmishing & artillery shelling occasionally. We were shelled a while early this morning. We and the enemy have been otherwise quiet except a few miles higher up the lines when Longstreet drove them back. They have just sent in a flag of truce & drove them back. They have just sent in a flag of truce & the skirmishing has certainly ceased. I suppose it is to bury their dead. Only one man was hurt in my co. I haven't heard a word from you since Ken left. Suppose it is the mails to blame. Mr. Hamlin came to see Rob't the other day.

In haste
your affectionate son
CDM.

Camp near Morton's Ford
Friday Dec. 4th. 1863

My Dear Mother

I have had no opportunity to write since the late movements here & I know you are uneasy about me, especially as the papers contain so many accounts of the fight of Johnson's Division & c. I am in hopes you thought I was not in the fight, but I was & God has again preserved me. The whole army was in motion on Thursday the 26th. & Friday morning I joined the Division & that evening the enemy's advance came upon our flank as we were moving along the road five or six miles from here. Our Division fought the 3rd. (French's) army corps from 4 to 7. We drove them back some distance & that night we fell back to our line of battle. Our loss was about 500. The 25th. suffered very little. I had one man right severely wounded. We lay in line of battle until last Wednesday morning when it was discovered that the enemy was gone. The truth was we had the position on them & if they had fought us, they would have gotten terribly beaten. They have all gone back to the north side of the Rapidan & our army yesterday evening moved into its old position. We are in the same camp & everything indicates some stay here. I hardly think the Yankees will attempt another movement this winter. We had a right rough time but I got on as comfortably as any one else and am perfectly well. Church will meet again tomorrow I reckon & I expect I will stay at Mr. Sissons again. They are the kindest people you ever saw—treat me as a member of the family. The Yankees came in sight of his house Thursday evening week & I had to get out. I think they did not trouble him very much, tho I haven't been there since. I am anxious to hear from you haven't had a letter since Sunday week. I will write again when we get more settled. Mr. Propst will be down Monday or Tuesday or Wednesday next. However, I am not suffering at all for the coat &c.

With love to all
Charles

∽

Morris Island S.C.
Sept. 20th. 1864

My dear brother

    Some Dixie letters were rec'd last evening & I was disappointed that there was none for me. I somewhat looked for a reply to a letter I wrote Mother Aug. 3rd. from the Prison Ship off Hilton Head. Though I then dared not say so, I yet fully expected to see you ere this but "twas ever thus from childhood's hour". This hope deferred is making the heart sick. I see no more hope now for a speedy exchange when I did two months ago and yet I don't give up hope. We are on Morris Island, directly under fire of our batteries but they are too good marksmen to fire anywhere to do us harm. There is not the slightest occasion for uneasiness on your part. I would not exchange places with any other prisoner as I'm fully convinced the first exchanges will be at this point. We are in tents and comfortable & I am well and healthy.

With best love to all
Yr. afft. brother
C.D. McCoy

Letters Pertaining to William Kenneth McCoy

Sergeant,
Carrington's Charlottesville (Virginia) Artillery Battery
    Early's Division
    Ewell's Army Corps
    Army of Northern Virginia

William McCoy was the son of William McCoy and Sally Anne Kemper McCoy who made their home in Charlottesville, Virginia.

He was born January 31, 1843, and was a Sergeant in Carrington's Charlottesville (Virginia) Artillery Battery. He was wounded Sunday, May 3, 1863, at the Battle of Chancellorsville and died in Richmond, Virginia, 19 May 1863.

⁓

Camp near Hamilton's Crossing
May 11, 1863

Mrs. McCoy
Dear Madam

I wrote several days ago but everything has been in so much confusion here. I fear the letter was not sent and therefore deem it proper to again announce that your son was very seriously wounded in the recent engagement at Chancellorsville while he was conscientiously discharging his duty in a most manly way. I sympathize most deeply with you in this sad affliction. His gentlemanly deportment ever since we have been intimately associated together has caused me to form a warm attachment for him. I most correctly hope he will speedily recover. He was sent from this place to Richmond and I hope before this letter reaches you he will be safety at home. If so please give him my deepest sympathy.

Very respectfully,
James Carrington
Capt. Charlottesville Battery

Thursday morning
University, May 21, 1863

My dear only Brother

Was very hard for me to write today but I must write to you. We have nothing to do in Richmond now. We brought home that precious little brother yesterday and laid him between our two sweet sisters. I will tell you from the beginning as much as I can remember about him. Bessie has written to you twice. You know it will be two weeks tomorrow since we heard that he was wounded and that he had been taken to Richmond. The next day I went down not knowing how he was hurt. Roger Martin met me and told me that he was badly wounded but that it was hoped he would recover. He went with me at once to see him; he was in the Officer's Hospital where everything was very nice. A great many ladies who knew him or knew of him had been to see him and had carried him every delicacy. Tho his eyes were closed and his whole face was covered with cotton I found him quite cheerful and hopeful. He said he had a right good appetite. He asked directly about all at home and when we heard from you and said "I am so thankful that Charley was not in that battle; it was an awful fight." I stood with him a good while and then went with Roger to the rooms of the Christian Association to write to mother. I then went back to him and stood until half past 9 o'clock. Frank Bibb was lying in bed next to him and two other officers each with a leg amputated were in the other side of the room. Bibb's nurse and a white servant were with him doing everything that was necessary, so I determined to go home with Roger and make arrangements to move him to his house early in the morning. He asked me to read and pray with him before I went; I read the 41st. Psalm and prayed; then told him goodnight. In the morning I got everything ready and secured temporary medical attendance. As we carried him along in a stretcher on that bright Sabbath morning, the church bells were ringing; he said to Roger "Mr. Martin I am keeping you from church. I wish I could go to church." We fixed him on a lounge with a hard mattress in the parlor; he said directly that he felt so much more comfortable there and was glad he had been moved. Dr. Lems an eminent surgeon soon came and examined him and said all his symptoms were hopeful. He slept easily the greater part of Sunday and that night; but when he was awake talked very pleasantly with me and with Roger's sisters. Grace teased him a little about Sue M.P. and asked him if she was not his sweetheart. He said rather sadly "she used to be Miss Grace but I have not got any now." On Monday, by putting simple lerate and linseed oil on his face I was able to move all the cotton & flim and found to my joy that his face would not be at all scarred. His eyes were still closed with matter but during the day he got them partially open and exclaimed with a quick voice and in a pleased manner "Lord I can see light". It was the first day of light he had had for eight days. He said afterwards that when he was first wounded he did not expect to live five minutes, and thought all his face was blown away. I asked him if it was his business to cut the "fuse". He said everything was his business that there were not men enough to work the guns and that if he had to oversee it all and the man whose business it was to cut the fuse was awkward. He told me that they had driven the enemy two miles before he was wounded, half a mile of it at a trot and that they were then only 500 yrds. from the enemy's batteries. He said the shell were falling so much around him that he did not know whether he was wounded by his own shell or by the enemy's. He saw only a flash. His clothes were all torn or burned off of him. He called for someone to put out the fire, but in the war of battle it was some minutes before he was noticed. Then Mr. Marshall of Barboursville came to him, but did not recognize him at first. Wilbur Davis took him to a spring and poured water on him and gave him water to drink for three hours. Then he was put in a fly tent on some blankets where he lay Wednesday evening when he was taken in a broken ambulance and put on the cars at "Hamilton's Crossing" and after many delays got to Richmond at one o'clock Thursday night. He had sent his tin plate to Young Dodd to bring home. I will return to the first Monday in Richmond. That morning Roger got Dr. James Bolton who is considered the best surgeon in the city and who is appointed to attend officers only to come and see him. He kindly gave me a note to the Gen.'s hospital, requesting that he should be transferred to him and promising to attend him tho' he was already over burdened with patients. He said he thought he would get well without the loss of a limb. We cannot be too thankful to that kind, gentle, attentive and skillful man. He did everything that man could do. Monday afternoon the wound in his arm bled about a pint I think; it exhausted him very much and alarmed me.

As Dr. Bolton was not in touch I sent urgently for Drs. Lewis &Cummingham; they both came and John thought that he could not recover. Dr. B. came at night and thought him doing well. But I had already telegraphed mother & Bessie and was assured that they could be there the next evening. When I told him they were coming he was very glad but asked for a little morphine as he was afraid he would be too much excited, said he only wanted to see them a few minutes that night and then go to sleep and be bright the next morning to talk to them. When they came he asked me not to let mother touch him when she came in talked pleasantly with them and then told them he wanted them to go to bed and rest for they were tired. I felt a little hopeful about him then. I did not take off any clothes while I was with him; I slept a few hours sometimes on a pallet, getting up at short intervals to see about him or to do something, therefore there was always someone in the room. I dressed his wounds very often myself except the one on his arm. I bathed them constantly and generally gave him his medicine and food. Hundreds of times did he call "Brother Henry" to do something for him. He never forgot to say "thank you" for anything that was done for him. He will always be a sweet remembrance to me that I nursed him with constant devotion and with intense yearning love and that he appreciated it so gratefully and lovingly. He seemed to be doing well until Friday and Sat. when his left leg, which seemed to be only a little bruised began to pain him very much and indeed he was in an agony as he expressed it all over. Then we had to give him morphine more frequently which made him dream a great deal and talk in his sleep. His dreams were decoherent and mostly of the battle field and his company; he drilled them sometimes calling "Halt!" giving orders about taking out his piece; called the men's names very often. Once he said "You must excuse me gentlemen, I can't engage in this game. I forgot I can't see nor use either hand nor walk a step; I am badly wounded". Once he called you "Charley, Charley McCoy" and when told you were not there he said he "thought some one said your regiment had been ordered back". His mind was perfectly calm and clear in the midst of all his suffering. We could wake him at any moment and he was perfectly himself, his manner, his language, his gentleness and politeness which he never forgot for a moment. He devised a machine for raising of the bed and for propping him up. He was ready with a reason for everything he said. His patience and meek submission to the will of God were perfectly beautiful. Often during the day and the night when he had a little respite from pain, he would ask me to "give him a drink of water and then pray a short prayer with him. He almost always said "Amen" at the close of it. He said in his sleep "I do try from the bottom of my heart" mother asked, What? he said "to trust in God and in Jesus Christ". Once he said "I do hate to hear you talk so boy; oh how you will repent it some of these day" Mother asked what? he said "Risk is cursing & swearing and I have tried to persuade him to stop it". On Sunday about two o'clock he was suffering very much and after a while said he wanted to collect his thoughts and wanted brother Henry to pray with him. Then he began himself "Oh Lord for Jesus Christ's sake, give me a little ease from my pain that I may collect my thoughts and pray to thee" (and then as if that prayer were answered he proceeded) "Oh Lord for Jesus Christ's sake, pour out upon me of the Holy Spirit and make me a thorough Christian; and if it be considered with thy holy will, give me this night refreshing sleep that with the light of tomorrow morning I may wake to worship thee in spirit and in truth; and bless all these dear ones around me and may we all meet at last around thy throne in heaven for Jesus's sake, "Amen". It was pronounced in a deliberate, sweet voice! It was so solemn, so beautiful. On the Wed. night before as mother was telling him goodnight he said "Mother, don't forget to pray for me before you go to sleep, pray that God will forgive all my wickedness, pray that Jesus will be with me, that he will abide with me in sickness and in health". Once when his lips were quivering with pain and I was telling him how I felt for him he said "But I will be glad of all this suffering when it is over if it brings me nearer to Jesus and makes me a more thorough Christian". Dr. Wm. Hope happened to be in town and sent him word that he was going to see him Thursday evening; he told me that he would not take morphine until after Dr. Hope came if he could help it—that he wanted to feel bright then. I told him Dr. Hope would make allowance for him. He said "I know that but oh, I want to have a little talk with him; he has always admired Dr. Hope very much" but his visit was deferred until Kenny had given him up and had taken his morphine about half an hour before he came; he was too drowsy to talk much but listened as well as he could to the singing of two sweet verses of "Jesus lover of my soul" and to the words of instruction and comfort and to the prayer but it was too protracted for him & he said after Dr. Hope went out "I was very glad to see Dr. Hope but am sorry he stayed so long". I will give you an assistance of his ready reasoning powers; all food was distasteful to him; I was giving him some egg nog the morning before his death and when he had nearly finished it I asked him to take the rest as there was only a little. He instantly replied "well if there is only a little it is not important that I should take it". Once when mother thought him asleep she said mournfully "we shall see him go soon"—He heard it and said, "If I was ready I would not care how soon I went", mother said where? he replied "to Heaven". Last Monday about 12 P.M. he had a violent nervous chill with pulpitation at the heart. He said it was only nerves, that he was not cold. After that time he had an occasional hiccup and we felt scarcely a ray of hope for his recovery, but Dr. Bottom said it was not impossible, that we must do everything we could and leave the rest with God; he was in great pain and called me every few minutes that day and night to put my hands under his hips & back and lift him a little off the bed. Monday night he told Sam (the servant) that he would "give him $3.00 to sit up with him that night and "let brother Henry rest". He so often said he was sorry to make me so much trouble and that I should have such and many things to do for him. He wanted me to take some of the stimulants which were provided for him because he said it was almost as necessary for me as for him. On Tuesday morning Miss Grace heard him say in his sleep "All for Jesus" & little after three o'clock Tuesday afternoon I noticed that his breathing was much more difficult and sent in haste for the Dr. but it soon became easy—at a quarter to 4 Taylor who had been with us a few days left and 5 minutes afterwards I raised Kenneth's head and gave him half a tumble of eggnog, he drank it and I asked if he would have some water (as he usually did after taking anything). He said just distantly enough for me to understand "I can't take it"—

slight. On the same day, in the afternoon, another telegram informed us that he was in Richmond. I went down on Saturday (2 weeks ago today) and found him at the "Baptist Female Institute" hospital, which is for officers only. Lieut. Bibb who is badly wounded, had been taken there with him. I expected to bring him home the next day but found him so dreadfully injured that I could only move him on a stretcher as far as my friend Roger Master's about a mile from the hospital. I secured the constant attendance of Dr. Botton (who is considered the most eminent surgeon in the city) besides the occasional attendance of several others. He was wounded at 10 o'clock on Sunday morning by the explosion of a shell in his own hands. He was cutting the fuse at the time; and it is supposed that it was ignited by some of the numerous explosions around him. He told me, he did not know whether it was his own shell or one from the enemy, that struck him as they were falling all around him. His face was burned all over but would have not been scarred if he had lived. When I first saw him it was entirely covered with cotton so that no feature could be seen, but I soon got it off. He did not see a ray of light for eight days, but on Monday I got his eyes open so that he could see a little. His hands were terribly burned and mangled several fingers were broken. Three of them partly gone. His clothes were either torn or burnt off. He had a very bad burn on the right groin and another very deep and nearly as large as my hand, a little lower down, on the same thigh. Just above the right knee was a bad shell wound nearly as large as my hand and in part of it nearly or quite to the bone. But his worst wound was in the left arm—the under part about 3 inches from the shoulder. A part of the flesh nearly or quite as large as my fist was removed but neither the bone nor the artery were broken. His symptoms were hopeful until Monday afternoon (11th.) when the wound under his arm bled about a pint and weakened him very much. I at once telegraphed to Mother & she and Bessie came the next day. The Doctor thought him doing well again until last Monday (though he had suffered an agony of pain on Saturday and Sunday) when he had a violent nervous chill. After that I had hardly any hope of his recovery. On Tuesday about 3 o'clock afternoon I saw that he had great difficulty of breathing, & sent at once for the Dr. Ten minutes before 4 o'clock, I gave him half a tumbler of eggnog according to the Dr.'s previous direction. He swallowed it right well, and I asked him if he would have some water (which he always wanted after taking anything). He said just distinctly enough for me to understand him, "I can't take it." At that same moment I saw that his eyes were fixed. His breathing was as gentle as an infants, and at 4 o'clock he was gone.

It was all the work of our Heavenly Father & he doeth all things well but it is a chastening that has broken our hearts. He was the darling of the family, and as a son, and brother, was all that we desired. We have not a doubt that he is happy now with his Father and Sisters, before the throne of God, his Father and Redeemer. God has mingled so much grace with affliction. About the last of April he had written to Mother that he hoped his prayers for her were in a measure answered and that God had changed his heart. He professed a delight in prayer & the scriptures that he never felt before, and he was resolved never to turn back. He has for a very long time been serious & prayerfull. During the ten days that I was with him, he would often during the day and night when he felt a little easier, say "Brother Henry give me a drink of water & then pray with me if you please—a short prayer." I never saw such a spirit of patience & submission in my life. He never uttered a murmer of a groan and was so far from regretting that he had been in that battle that he would not have been any where else. He thought he had only done his duty. And yet, the first night that I saw him he said "he was so thankful that Charlie was not in that battle, that it was an awful fight. He described the battle to me up to the time

62

he was wounded and said they had already driven the enemy two miles. His manner, his voice, his politeness were all his own to the last. He never forgot to say thank you for anything that was done for him. He was in a constant spirit of prayer & faith. Once when he was suffering very much and I wanted to do something to relieve him, he said "I will be glad if all this, when it is over, if it only brings me nearer to Jesus and makes me more thorough Christian. In his sleep he said, "All for Jesus" & Lord for Jesus Christ's sake, and many such things. Once when he was in great pain, he prayed that God would give him a little ease, that he might collect his thoughts & pray; & there as if his prayers were answered, he proceeded to utter the most beautiful prayer I ever heard. But I cannot tell you all now. We try to thank God for his mercies in this affliction and as it was his will that he should be taken from us now, we should have preferred that very way, in which God took him. His death was that of a willing, glorious martyr by the side of Genl. whom he had always followed. He never knew of Jackson's death. We brought him up on Wednesday, and laid him between Mary & Sue. I thank you for all your kindness Uncle. I know you will all sympathize with us. Mother & Bessie send much love to you all. We thank you for writing so often. Your afft. nephew H.P.R.M.

My dear Mrs. McCoy:

I have heard with much pain and sympathy of your dear Kenneth's death. My sorrow is greater because I cannot go to you, and mingle my tears and prayers with yours at the mercy seat. Yet by faith we can meet there, and have. I have remembered our fellowship in Christ, and tried to bear you on my heart in my approaches to the throne. But I feel the weakness and poverty of our sympathy and intercessions. Only Christ can avail for such grief as yours. And be sure you are not without them. His hand created and intertwined those living fibres which bound your dear boy's heart to yours. He gave them their sensitiveness. His hand, too, it was, that severed them, suddenly, violently, yea it may sometimes appear, with needless, sevenity. Nay, not "needless". Do not think so. On the other hand is it not unspeakably blessed to know, to know that he has done all in faithfulness, in kindness, in love; with a hand of tendernest carefulness; with a heart overflowing with sympathy? What says the scripture? "Touched with the feeling of our informities;" "He himself hath suffered". Ah, then, when he allowed your poor boy's hands to be torn by the cruel iron, he had not forgotten his own hands lacerated by the cruel nails. And that wounded heart. It is still sensitive to the sufferings of the people, and quick to sympathize. Why persecutest thou Me? He cried, as if in anguish when his saints were persecuted. The names of his people are graven on the breast plate which ever lies upon his heart, and feels every movement of its infinite pity. Yea, we are members of his own body.

What more can we ask? What though we cannot fathom His purposes in these multiplied sorrows sent so rapidly on your little household? Can we not trust him in the thick cloud, the black night, the deep sea? Oh, let us try not only to submit to his will, but to adore it. I am sure he means well by you, by you all; yea, something very gracious. Ere long you shall see it, and be "saitisfied". Your sorrows shall be turned into joy; your trust, whether timed or showy, into vision clear and full of blessedness.

Let us try to live in faith of "that day". It will comfort and strengthen and cheer.

I remember with inexpressible pleasure my last "interview with your precious child. His placid features, his gentle patience, his meekness, and (I think I may say) his childlike faith, are all before me, and have left the sweetest image on my heart. I thank God I was enabled to meet his deep desire to see me and convene with me.

This hasty letter is to you all. The God of all comfort be with you.

Sincerely your brother in Christ,
William J. Hope

༄

Camp near Guiney's Station, Va.
June 3rd. 1863

Mrs. McCoy

Will not, we trust, consider it an intrusion upon the sacred privacy of parental grief, for us, the Messmates of her lamented son, Kenneth, to unite our voices in bearing testimony to his worths and to mingle our tears of heartfelt sympathy and sorrow over his honored and but too early grave. The relations into which we were thrown, and the ties of community of interest, community of sentiment and feeling, community of action and of suffering by which we were bound to him, we believe to have been second in intimacy and affection only to those of home itself. Out off from relatives and friends and dependent upon each other for society and sympathy, while we shared daily the same fare and occupied nightly the same shelter, our Mess. had grown into a family circle.

What, at the outset, had been acquaintanceship had blossomed into friendship and ripened into mature affection. In him our hitherto unbroken circle has lost its first link, and we feel as though a brother had been struck down from our midst.

As we look back upon the past we can scarcely realize the fact that he who was to so large an extent the light and life of our bonds, has past away from earth that we shall never see again the genial smile of his bright face or hear the animated tones of his cheerful voice. In our constant and unreserved intercourse with him for the closing year of his life, amid scenes which are universally admitted to "try men's souls" and to develop defects which would pass unnoticed in the occasional intercourse of more peaceful times. We can remember no single instance, in words or acts, which could detract in the smallest degree from the character of the high toned gentleman.

On the contrary, the more we knew of him, the more we loved him.

We love him for his kind and obliging disposition, his warm and affectionate heart. The vivacity and buoyancy of his spirits, and the frankness, generosity, unaffected simplicity and real nobility of his true nature. We remember with joyful sadness the elevated morality which shaped his conduct, his freedom from the innumerable petty faults as well as the grosser vices which stain the character of so many by his age. Above all we remember his habitual reverence for sacred things, his constant attendance on our occasional prayer meetings and his frequent reading of the Words of Life.

Several of our members are professed followers of the meek and lowly Jesus, and in our wanderings had endeavored in our feeble way to set up a family alter. In this none took a deeper and more lively interest than Kenneth.

For some time before his wounds were received he seemed to take a deeper interest in all religious exercises than ever before, and he expressed on several occasions the desire and intention of joining the church the first opportunity that presented itself.

In the hurried march on the day previous to the battle at Chancellorsville he kept open in his hand and read at every halt a little book, the property of one of us composed of verses selected from the Bible.

It is impossible to reflect without keen regret upon the untimely blighting of so many budding hopes, the cruel disappointment of so noble a promise.

We find comfort in the assurance that he could have fallen in no nobler cause, that the messenger of death found him at the post of duty—joy, in the hope that our loss, which is temporary, is his eternal gain.

And while, notwithstanding these considerations, we still wish it had been otherwise, we would strive to bow in humbel, trusting submission to the will of "him who doeth all things well." "Even so, Father, for so it seemed good in thy sight."

With great respect and heartfelt sympathy

W.F. Davis
A.B. Roler
D. Glanson Boyden
R.W. Lewis, Jr.
Albert L. Holladay
S.L. Marshall
P.G. Wash
T.M. Swoope

This Yankee stationery was captured by William Kenneth McCoy.

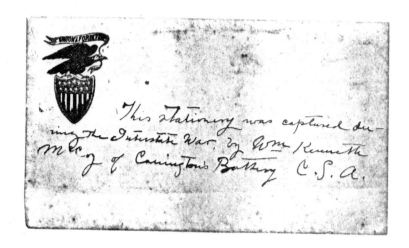

Letters with Regard to Charles Thomas Shelton

Private
Co. H, 28th Virginia Infantry
  Botetourt (Virginia) Artillery Battery and
  Anderson's Artillery Battery
  Maney's Tennessee Brigade

Charles Thomas Shelton was the son of David R. Shelton and Victoria Jackson Kean Shelton, who lived at "Roseneath" on the waters of Owens Creek, Louisa County, Virginia.

Camp at Centreville Oct. 26th. '62
Saturday

Dear ones at the home of my childhood,

I have but just received your dear little missive of love and remembrances penned by Lucy, yet speaking to my heart words of love and affection from all more dear to me than jewels or precious stones & it is a great pleasure to find myself at liesure to send back one word of love in return this evening. We seldom have liesure moments here now, and only, when resting after a long march or from work of some kind, and then Wm. Hughes & I have our own cooking to do, which consumes a good deal of the day. To day we have been comparatively free & it has brought back so vividly those school days now past forever. Our company is engaged in a game of Town Ball and my letters came, one from Lucy, the other from dear Hallie and I can now hear them a great glee over some fellow who has been so unfortunate as to feel the weight of the ball beneath his soldier jacket. The whole company, young & old are engaged in the game and this it is, which brings before me so vividly the school boy days when looked upon as disagreeable but which time teaches man is the happiest of his life. I think a great deal over the past in fact I occupy and amuse myself almost entirely with my thoughts for I have but very little society here since I

70

left the company. There are, it is true a great many kind hearted fellows but the moral stamina of the company is bad & they are not the kind I could ever choose for associates. Yes dear ones, many times at mid hour of night when you all perhaps are entirely unconscious of the world & what is doing therein. Sometimes while the rain falls in heavy torrents & you lie listening at the sweet and pleasant music as it falls upon the roof do my thoughts revert to you & home as I tread my lonely beat. Many times when exposed to the cold and rain do I ask myself the question are they thinking of me now! Yes, I know you do think of & sympathize with me & this it is that keeps me up. It is the thought of home that makes me able & willing to undergo any hardship. The weather has been very cold here for several days & we have had a great deal of rain with it which made our retreat from Fair. C.H. & the subsequent picket duty very disagreeable. We marched from the C.H. the retreat of the whole army and are now made to do most of the picketing which is terrible as we cannot have but one blanket, and are without tents or shelter of any kind besides sometimes they do not send us food & then we kill hogs if any are about but frequently have to fast. The enemy came up to the C.H. in large force but I understand that they have fallen back since that glorious victory at Leesburg (the most of the campaign) however we do not know whether it is true or not so many conflicting reports come to hand. We are now making some very formidable fortifactions at this place which with wood cutting and other duty keeps us all the time engaged, so that we are on some kind of duty every day. To give you an idea of what we have to do, two hundred men are detailed from this regiment for work tomorrow which by the way is Sunday. If Gen. McClellan comes this way he will wish he hadn't before he gets away but I don't believe that he will attack us here before the spring though everything indicates that our Gens.think differently. I understand that Uncle Walter is in the neigh-

Division Head Quarters
Fredericksburg, Va. 16th. Dec. 1862

Ma Chere Aime,

The times have been so full of excitement since the receipt of your last that I have been unable tho to give it an answer. My time when not spent in the discharge of my duties in the Q.M. Department has been given to the wounded of the late battles. I shall endeavor to give you some account of them and try to be as concise as possible; though events have been crowding upon each other in such quick succession and events of such great importance too, that I scarcely know how to begin or where to end. The most important have transpired in our division and the most of which I was eye witness. The long delay of the enemy to carry over execution their threat to shell the town of Fredericksburg began to make the citizens believe that they had abandoned their intentions of the work of destruction and make them feel that there be no iminent danger in remaining in town; consequently many families moved back again, although it was against the orders of Genl's Lee & Longstreet. On the morning of the 11th. inst about 5 o'clock the Yankees commenced their work of destruction. Our brigade (Genl. Barksdales) was on picket at the time and sent word to the commander of the signal and to give the alarm that the enemy were turning across their pontoon bridges. He prevented them from crossing until late in the evening at which time he received orders from Genl. Lee to fall back and let them come over. We reticated then to the upper portion on the town near the Markerhouse where our men found some protection or rather a screen from the enemy who were advancing up the same street in quite a large force. Genl. Barksdale ordered his men to hold their fire until the enemy came up very close to them and pour a deadly volley into their ranks which they did effectively. A close combat then ensued into the streets which resulted in the enemy getting most terribly whiped and being compelled to "skeedaddle" back to their river where they were placed under the protection of their batteries. During the time our men were driving them back from the opposite side of the river (before any had crossed at all) and keeping them from finishing their bridges, they were subjected and full exposed to a most raking, terrific fire of the enemy's batteries which were planted about in spots on every hill in sight. In the meantime the city was being shelled and burned. They seemed to aim their shells in the neighborhood of the churches. Two of them have been burned and also quite a number of buildings; yet there is a considerable portion of the old town left. I had a lady friend, two of them, and a gentleman, who were in town when the bombardment commenced. I loaned them the ambulance to go into town to stay, although I opposed them going and tried to dissuade them from doing so. I tell you I worked like a trojan to get them out. They were no less than Miss Millie's father, mother and aunt. Although I failed in my efforts, they however managed to get out safely and on hearing of my exertions in their behalf, she (Mrs. H) pronounced the benediction "God bless him". She was told that I had left the Q.M. Department and had gone to my company to participate in the fight. So grateful was she for my good intentions she walked half a mile to ascertain, leaving word that I was to be sent to her, if wounded and brought to the hospital. The mother saw me and expressed as much joy at meeting me as if I had been "her own son", not knowing that I hope to be at some future day. Miss M. has failed to tell her. Ought not I to do so? Give me your opinion and Counsin Matts too. Answer me unequivocally. But to continue the history of the battles. Romance is leading me astray. On the morning of the 12th. the enemy renewed their attack upon the city but did not keep it up very long as our forces were out of the town and beyond the reach of their guns. They then commenced throwing their troops across the river in large bodies and as rapidly as in their power. As they crossed they marched at a double quick down the rail-road and in the direction of Bowlgreen to get from with the range of our cannon which were throwing shell most beautifully into their ranks making great gaps as they exploded. Towards evening all was quiet except an occasional gun from the Yankee's side of the river who threw a shell into the uper part of the town where a few citizens were lying to make their escape into the country. On the night of the 11th. I saw no less than sixty or eighty women and children who had fled under the cover of darkness having concealed themselves all day in a cellar. On the night of 12th. the enemy were allowed to arrange their troops and plant their batteries. Having taken their positions they reversed their cannonading the following morning the 13th. at day break. About sunrise they sent forward their skirmises supported by their infantry. They were promply met by our forces and stood and contested the ground for an hour or more, when they were compelled to retreat. But they only retreated to bring up reinforcements treble our number. But our reinforcements were sent as promptly to meet them. On our right they over powered us once or twice, but in every instance we recovered our ground, and in the evening drove back both of their wings. A prettier place for a battle could not have been found. It is in the valley below the city. I was during the entire engagement standing on a high hill (Fall Hill) watching with intense interest the whole fight. You should have seen the way the Yankees run. You would there have some idea of the meaning of their favorite word "Skeedaddle". The position that I was in however, was rather dangerous. Picket's division being in trenches on the hill the enemy were constantly throwing shell at them. Just to my left where stands an old mill, was the Washington Artillery, whose position the enemy seemed not to like very much. They were on an elevation of about fifty feet above the town. From this position they nearly destroyed totally every regiment the Yankees sent to attack the forces in front of them and did completely demoralize them. So deadly was their force that they (Yankees) turned four of their batteries upon them and sent two brigade to charge upon it. Genl. McLaws very promptly sent in reinforcements; but before they could get where they would be of any service this artillery sent such a hail of grape, shell and canister, that they turned and fled in utter confusion. There was not a line to be seen. They looked like black birds flying over a ploughed field. Just at dusk they made a second attempt to take the same battery. They turned all of their guns from every battery upon them and sent forward five Brigades to take it. There was in an instant one constant war of artillery from every point on our side which together with our musketry drove them back after a very short engagement. Night set in and closed the scene, much to the great joy of many tired and wearied soldiers, who had been engaged in the hotest of the fight since early dawn. The wounded now commenced to groan and call aloud for help. Our wounded were all brought off of the field, secured proper attention and sent to Richmond for better nursing than they can receive here. The ladies here have been exceedingly kind and attentive to the wounded. They go into their tents (every house is filled with refugees) and nurse them and that well. The Yankees have been trying all day to throw some shells into our camps but without success. They are retreating, so I learn this morning. They entered private houses in Fredericksburg and took all of the furniture, bed clothes, clothing, flour, preserves, jelly, and such like that the citizens left behind not failing to chop up their pianos, bureaus and such furniture as they could not carry. Love to all. Am well & hearty. Write soon to your Sincere friend James W. Beaty

My dear Father:

We left Knoxville about three weeks ago & have been marching ever since until two days ago when we arrived at this place & I had hoped that we would now have some rest but that is out of the question for we are ordered to march again tomorrow. Whither I do not know but expect we will commence the onward to Nashville. On our route here we had a terrible time for the night before we commenced the ascent of the Cumberland Mountain a hard rain set in & beside drenching us put the roads in a very bad condition & after we struck the foot of the mountain it took us upwards of eight hours to travel a mile & a half. Sometimes we had sixteen horses to a gun & they could not turn a wheel. All the time the rain was pouring in torrents & with the rugged sides of a mountain to climb you can guess what a time we had. We were entirely exposed to three days hard rain & besides there came a heavy fall of snow which now lies on the ground. It is now 6th. Dec. & we are without tents & I do not suppose we will have any this winter. I have much cause to be thankful that I still retain my health, especially when I see so many strong men giving away before the exposure they have to undergo.

We have a splendid battery now and should we get into a fight (which seems very probable from the preparation) we will no doubt do good service. It is true that this division has done no fighting yet but Jackson's men have never done the marching nor seen the hardships that we have. In the last few months we have marched over 1500 miles & been half starved while marching it. My hands are so cold now that I can hardly hold this pencil and I must stop. You all must write to me when you can. Give my best love to Ma & the girls. I am with sincere affection your son.

Charles

In camp near Vicksburg
24th. Jan. 63

My dear Father

Let me congratulate you. I received a letter from Hallie a few days ago in which she informed me of the advent of my little sister of whose coming I have had not the slightest suspicion until the reception of a letter from Billy about Xmas. I have often heard you say that you did not want to hear any more babies cry at Roseneath but I am willing to bet two to one that you are today the proudest man in Louisa County. Now you need not think that I am at all envious for indeed I am not so. I am but too happy that at any rate such will not be my fortune during the war. Tell Ma she had better give the baby to Hallie as she already has seven daughters.

On yesterday morning the quiet of this vicinity was disturbed by the appearance of the enemy's gun boats and an almost countless number of transports in the river a few miles above the city. They seem to be landing their troops on the Louisiana side for what purpose I cannot imagine unless it is to try and cross the river below here. Certain it is, however, that they mean mischief and that they will attack Vicksburg in a few days. We all are very confident that they will be severely repulsed tho' whenever they undertake that job and feel not in the least alarmed at their demonstrations. Our guns on the river gave them several salutes yesterday but they were too far off to be much annoyed by us and finally they were allowed to land quietly. I do hope that some change will soon take place in order that we may get out of Miss. I never saw such a climate in mylife and am afraid that it will go hard with us Virginians to remain here during the summer. It rains here almost incessantly, and the mud in these low grounds is in a good many places knee deep. I do not exajurate at all when I say that we have three rainy days to one clear one. This portion of the army is a great deal worse fed than any I suppose in the confederacy. One of the butchers told me that frequently they had to lift up the cattle brought here for beef. I know they are poorer than I ever saw your cattle in the spring after an unusually hard winter. I had no idea before I was a soldier that a man could stand so much or live so well with so few of the luxuries of life. Hard as our fare is I am as fat and healthy as I ever was in my life but I am very much afraid of the fever and ague & therefore am very anxious to get away from Miss. Now with best love for the girls & Ma with a kiss for baby I am with much love and affection.

Your son,
Charles

Direct Vicksburg, Miss.

Camp Warrenton near Vicksburg
Monday April 27th., '63

My dear Father:

We expect to go some miles below here tomorrow on a sort of picket expedition to guard a boat landing & as it is altogether uncertain whether I will have the opportunity to write soon I will embrace the present liesure hour to perform this pleasant duty tho I fear from present rumors that my letter is not destined to reach you for some time. I allude to rumors now in circulation that the enemy has made a successful raid in our rear & destroyed a considerable portion of the railroad near or at Meridian however, as I have heard conflicting rumors I shall hope until further confirmation that they are all untrue. As all eyes are now turned on Vicksburg, I suppose you would like to hear how things are working out here. I am very much afraid that we have had some cause to feel discouraged within the last week or two. The enemy have successfully run our batteries with both transportation & gun boats on two separate occasions & last night from the heavy firing in the direction of Vicksburg. I suppose they ran by again. We sunk & disabled a good many boats to be sure but then my humble opinion is that the river might be so obstructed as to let none pass. There seems to be a screw loose somewhere. Their object in getting their boats below is evidently to attack this place or Port Hudson one or the other. In either case, I am confident of our ability to drive them back.

I have been very much disappointed in not hearing from John Richardson before this. At one time I had fondly hoped that I would soon be in old Virginia again but now begin to fear that I am to be sadly disappointed. You, dear father, who have never been departed for any length of time from your wife cannot know how my heart yearns almost to madness once more to see & be with her still you can & I know do readily sympathize with me in these trials. I think that I have been treated badly in this company or I would have seen you all long before this. The favorite ones have all been sent home under some pretext or other tho' some of them only joined the company while we were in Richmond. This is the reason or one of the reasons why I am so anxious to get a transfer. Capt. Johnston has positively refused to give any of us a transfer & my only chance to get out of the company is by getting an appointment of some kind & I do most earnestly hope that John has succeded in procuring the situation for me in his company. I had rather be with him than with any one else. I was very much surprised to learn that Uncle William had employed a substitute. He is one of the last I expected to hear of leaving the service. I am heartily sick of this war and long for my home & its loved ones as much as any one could do but it is my intention to stand by my post unless disabled to the last. I look upon it as the most incumbent duty which with God's help I shall perform to the best of my ability. Now, dear father, I approach a subject that I hardly know how to converse upon even with you. Yesterday I went to the 30th. Ala. Regt. to hear preaching & I was so much impressed with the sermon that it has led me to reflect or rather begin to reflect in the carelessness & wickedness of my past life. I hardly know how to describe my feelings. I do not feel any acute conviction of sin. I do not as yet feel as I think I should but the sermon which was very plain & pointed has led me to resolve with God's help to endeavor to lead a different life. Oh! if I could but feel more concerned about my salvation. I can only pray that I may feel aright. Will you dear father, now pray that I may be led to Jesus & accepted by him? I have resolved to read my Bible regularly & such religous matters as I can get hold of here in camp to leave off sinful habits as much as I can. May God strengthen my purpose & grant that I may be brought to him by the saving grace of Jesus Christ.

How are you getting along in the farming line? I suppose that you will not attempt much of a crop of tobacco this year but will comply with the president's request & raise principally corn & wheat. I hope that a large crop of bread stuffs will be made. I have heard very favorable reports of the crops so far. And now dear father with very best love for each & all at home I will bid you good bye. I am with much love & affection your son.

Charles

Hospital Vicksburg
May 5th. '63

Dear Father:

Before this reaches you you will have learned the result of the battle of Bayou Pierre how our small force held ten times their number in check all day. Our battery suffered severely—we lost four of our guns. I send a list of killed & wounded. I was slightly wounded in right hand & therefore have to write with my left. I thank God that I escaped with my life. My best love to all.

Affectionately your son
Charles T. Shelton

Envelopes from Letters of Charles T. Shelton

Envelopes from Letters of Charles T. Shelton

Letters Pertaining to John Taylor Anderson

Private,
Co. C, 13th Virginia Infantry
Gordonsville Grays

Smith's Brigade	Pegram's Brigade
Early's Division	Early's Division
Army of Northern Virginia	Army of the Shenandoah

Miss Sallie F. Anderson
Gordonsville Va
in the care of Mr Davis

Harpers Ferry Virginia
April 26, 1861

Dear Sister

We are all well at this time and as I have a few moments to spare I will write to you to let you know something of a soldiers life The greatest quantity of Ladies received many cheers and bouquets after a long and tiresome ride. we arrived at Harpers Ferry overnight. many cheer for the soldiers. Well as you know nothing about the life of a soldier I must begin at the first. Well as eating is the first thing we will commence to that we eat three meals on a plate (and all that is in it I tell you but no more) we eat what is set before us and ask no questions three hundred in one room (thick as pups) but make out very well. no one out of camp after dark if you do you are in the guard house before the time you can say Jack Robinson, several of our company have been in but I have kept clear.

The music is passing the window now I pause to listen, the sweetest that ever rung in the ear of a soldier, we can go anywhere we chose in the day time if not on duty, I have not yet been on. I have been over the bridge to Maryland mountains on every side picket guards on every nob for three miles every side (Charley is over in Maryland on picket guard today). every night at nine O'clock we are called out in the street and the roll is called then brake ranks and return immediatly. last evening Capt Scott gave orders to be in readiness in a moments warning muskets and equipment. the next morning about 5 O'clock the drum commenced sounding to arm! to arms! was the cry from the captin one minute we were in the battlefield as we supposed but had no fight. we

86

stood for about two hours muskets and bayonets glittering with the honor of Virginia all we wanted was the sight of a yankee. the blood would no doubt have covered the ground and even stood in ponds but no enemy approached. the same morning we took up General A army as he was passing on the train he was covered up under some sheets in the baggage car but his lodging is now in the guard house. Well this is Sunday morning I commenced your letter friday morning but not being to finnish it as I was called to the picot guard on Friday morning and not relieved until today. I did not have but one blanket and one of them had none I gave him half of mine so it was very bad sleeping too to one blanket on the top hole of a mountain without any cover . . . . . . and having to stand guard 6 or eight hours during the time but made out tolrably well untill the morning when It commenced raining so hard it was very bad. My feet are still soaking wet halfway up to my knees no fire at all and a very hard and nasty place to sleep in the camp or on the batle field sister I must close and proberly the last letter you will ever receive from me. may God enable you to pray continuously for me tell Pap it is write rough and tell him to remember son in his prayers I have not much time to read but can pray even in the battle field my love to all in the neighborhood all the little ones and tell little kittie Goodby and to sweet one in heaven where parting is no more. may the good lord take care of you

your affectionate bro J T Anderson

To S F Anderson

PS if you write by mail direct it in the care of Captain Scott Harpers Ferry Jefferson Co.

Gordonsville Grays, Company C, 13th Va Infantry under Col. J.A. Walker

Harpers Ferry (Va)
May 6th 1861

Dear Sister

I received your kind and affectionate letter yesterday and with a heart full to overflowing. I perused its contents. it carried me back to the old but loved place (home) where we were reared up from childhood on my way to manhood—but I never thought we should part and be thrown in the mist of strife and conflict but that time has arrived when from around the fire side (where once all was find and wonderful & love) there is a brother gone when the chairs are not around the table there is absent one and the loved ones look and sight about but we leave them in the hands of God. He can take care of them and be as a brother or father or husband and bless them with eternal life. Sister I received the close you sent I am very much obliged to you they will be of great use to me, we have a very good barracks now. we have the Church had preaching yesterday morning in the church and they had the Sunday school in the eve. we will be meeting next wednesday night. I dont know how long we will stay here not long I dont think but the general idea is that we shall remain here twelve monthes or more but do not think so. some think we shall have an attack soon. we dont know and dont care much, we had as live fight as not. we heard that old Capt Scott says he intends to have this place if it takes the last man he has and Major Jackson says he will kill the last man here before he gets it so you may listen for the report of my musket if an attack is made. about six hundred troops from Kentucky came in the other day.they look sorter like fighting men I tell you they certainly arent afraid of no one . . . but they say if you put them on top of the mountain they can kill every yankee that gets in there way. I think they will fight pretty hard from their looks. They came by Gordonsville I recon you have heard of them tell sis jinnie I had my picture taken on sheet iron the other day I had my musket and two pistols it looked rite savage I sent it to cousin Fannie Gay. I recon it will friten her very much as she dont like to talk about war. I did not write anything just slipped the picture in and directed it to her. I thought it was no time to be talking about nothing don't tell sis. Have you received any letters for me if you have and if you have a convenient way you can send them to me if not you can answer them and tell them just to wait until I got things strate and I will wait on them with the greatest facility but tell them not to pester me when I am settling difficulties between Nations. if you send your letters by mail you must direct them in the care of Cap Scott of the Gordonsville Grays I must close goodbye may God be with you always even until the end

Your devoted Bro
(John Taylor Anderson)

Box 5 Miss Sallie F Anderson
Gordonsville Va
Care of Jesse Anderson

Harpers Ferry (Va)
May 16 1861

Dear Sister

    I received your kind and welcome letter to day and with much pleasure and interest I read its contents it made me feel like I was at home even at home breathing the fine air that is over whistling around the old but ever loved home. I received the bundle of clothes & cakes.

Sallie we had a very hard and tiresome march the other day to Sheperdtown about twelve miles through the rain & sleet and mud a brief description of wich you will find in Nannies letter and as you can read it there I will not take up my time in describing it now. Some say it was an over look in the Officers that we had to go for they could have sent one of the troopers out there and back in two hours and all would have been wright. several men are sitting around me writing to there but think we have plenty of artillery here also plenty of men to hold harpers old ferry. some say there is eleven thousand men here but I dont think there is more than seven or eight. we have some of the Kentucky and Alabama boys with us, the soldiers are coming in every day. I will close Give my love to all and except any wishes from your affectionate Brother JTA

(John Taylor Anderson)

To Gordonsville

Harpers Ferry
June 7th 1861

Dear Sister

I will try to write you a little more about the nice box of provisions which you sent. The box came to hand today with all the provisions spoiled except Jinnies cake and the pickle and butter, the socks were not short (sister dont say anything about it at all) my feelings were very much mortified when I burst the nice box open and found it spoiled but it could not be helped not that I craved the good eating

90

so much but me missing such a nice treat from the loved ones at home but dont say anything about it. I was very much obliged to you all for your kindness but I wont eat all of my treat now. I have my bucket of butter which I will enjoy finely (it taste so good) tell Miss Lucy I am very much obliged to her & I will kill old uncle grandfather Abraham, if I can just see the white of his eyes once but if old Abe had seen me when I bit on one of those pickle there wouldnt have been any killing him (you know how pickle makes any body squinch up their face) well I must tell you something about our folks. we are all well with one or two exceptions Charly and myself have gotten intirely well. I believe I have not been on guard duty since I was sick but expect to go on tonight The boys are all well and fat and cheerful, think as much about fighting as if there never was such a thing as war. keep all in readiness though if an alarm was made at the stroke of midnight or any other time we would be marching in about two minutes. about our eating we have arranged things a great deal better we are divided off with sequads and draw open rations and have them cooked at the private houses about town there is six in my squad. we have one place it is a great deal better to set down at the table and eat and some good coffee than it was with us before the cooking cost us about $1 a month apiece. rather pay that than live as we have done before. the old lady cooks very well. Sallie I must close for tonight may lord protect us safely while we rest our weary bodies and close our eyes in slumber Good night. good morning Sallie (just from breakfast we had very hard drill this morning befoe breakfast but we are getting used to it. the regimental drill is great deal harder than the Company drill. it is so much longer to keep us standing still so much we have heard several times that we are going to move to Eastern Virginia but the majority of the Company prefers staying here. as for myself I greatly prefer staying here, it is very healthy here I think, we have not had more than one or two warm

Fairfax   Miss S F Anderson Gordonsville Orange Co.
                        Camp Fairfax Sept 4th 1861

Dear Sister

This evening finds me on the battlefield where we have a very good situation and pretty good fair. The camp is about a half a mile from the station. Our reg is on picit. at present I "dont" know when they will be in as it is uncertain when they go or come, we found several of our men here. The most of them sick. Well Sallie my trip yesterday wearied me somewhat; as it was about 9 O'clock last night when we arrived Roberson that was killed in our regiment while out skirmishing last week saw two Yankees about two or three hundred yards firing at them several times but as he fired the last time one of the two turned and shot him. he lived untill morning he beg them to kill him.

Well I must close as it is time to be getting it in the office. Give my love to all and except what you deserve from your devoted Bro John

To Gordonsville   Dec 5th 1861

The politeness of Capt Solman

Dear Sister

This morning finds me again among those who are standing in defence of their country and who are now batering against the cold winter nights. we are campt near Centreville but our post office is Manassas. we get the mail every day. there are about thirty Reg (as near as I can guess) encampt

93

near or in sight of this place. we arrived here Thursday morning we had a beautiful morning from Manassa down which is about seven miles. The weather is beautiful at this time except a bitte cold at night but we build a chimney to our tent yesterday which makes it quite comfortable except a little smoke some times. I am sitting by my little fire now it is very comfortable indeed much better than fire outside. I slept very well last night. There are four in our tent and ten in our mess. our eating has also improved very much. The fellows have learned to cook very well but I have got to learn yet this is my day to cook. I hope I can remain here during the winter. there is some talk about reintering for another twelve months but I dont think I shall for I think I can get some business where I can escape the malisha. well Sallie you must write directly you get this and give me all the news my love to all and tell Puss to write also

> remain your affectionate
> brother John T Anderson

PS Direct your letter to Manassa Junction 13th Reg Va Volunteer

> John T Anderson

⁓

to Gordonsville

> Camp Hill (Va) Dec 15, 1861

Dear Sister Sallie

I received your long kind letter last friday and was certainly very glad to hear from you. camp is quiet nothing going on of interest except throwing up breastworks they continue to throw them up but have gotten back to our digging trenches and throwing up breast works. there is some talk of our moving toward Manassa next week to take winter quarter. hope we may for it is so inconvenient about geting anything from anywhere to this place. hope we may get back to roads & the railroad where we can get anything from home we want during the winter. when we get into winter quarters I expect to send home more bad clothing. if I find I need them my comfort answers a very good purpose. I tell you these cold nights it certainly feels comfortable. Longstreets Division has gone into winter quarters. that is they have put them up some cohafs there with dirt and some with slabs. hope they will send us a load or two of planks to make beds if nothing else. I intended answering your letter this morning but concluded I would go over to the 19th R to see some of my friends and have just returned and concluded to write any how this eve for fear we might have to lieve tomorrow as there is some talk of it. the 19th Reg has build winter quarters. most of them will have them complete in about a week. well Sallie for a Christmas do you expect to spend or have you even thought of it at all. our Regiment has commenced Christmas and I believe or something worse the Sargent came to me the other night to take a sentinels place. he had been arrested for getting drunk and he was the first I think. about half of the Reg was drunk that night and all the next morning. Sallie you spoke of my prayers you certainly have them and I certainly wish you would pray for me for there is nothing on earth that I desire above a sisters prayers and I trust that by the assistance of God we may be enabled to pray aceptably for each thing if I ever believed in earnest in my life it was for your welfare in the future. Well Sallie I must close

I remain your
prayerful Bro
John (Taylor Anderson)

Dec 24th 1861

Dear Sister

I red your kind and very interesting letter yesterday which was read and perused with much care. Well Sallie we have moved since youve heard from us. we are now encampt in about two miles of Manassa and very busy building winter quarters. We had quit a stormy day yesterday it cleared of last night but very cold and the wind blowed so hard that we could not have any in our tents for smoke. We could get our quarters done this week if we had planks but it is doubtful about getting plank this week. Tell Uncle Wm Carter I think he can dispose of his plank by applying to the quartermaster at any price. I wish you would nit me a cap to sleep in. get Jimmie to give you some yarn and nit it in the shape of those nets cousin Pattie was nitting when I was there only have it thicker something like a comfort and send it in my Christmas box. How I would like to be with you this cold Christmas eve morning to help you eat pies. Tell Jinnie to send me some more sausage meat if she has plenty & Ties in my christmas box and you had better write me word when you are going to send it and meet the box at the junction. Well Sallie you said I must write you a long letter but you must excuse me this time for I am in a great hurry and very cold sitting here in the open tent without a spark of fire this Christmas eve. what a cold and blustering day it is but we must hope for the best. we are enjoying ourselves the best we can. dont expect to see any Christmas or even to know when it falls but I have been well ever since I left home. hope I will remain so for it is all I dread in the army being sick. I wrote to Mr. H. by Capt Scott and sent them five dollars in it. please write whether he sent it or not. Mr. Jones left this morning he is coming back the 7 of January next. hope he will bring some good books to read this winter. I wish so much that we were in our winter quarters we could make ourselves so much more comfortable than we have. well Sallie I must close you must write soon and remember always in your prayers your devoted Bro

John (Taylor Anderson)

❧

To Gordonsville
Camp Walker (Va) Jan 9th 1862

Dear Sister Sallie

Your very interesting letter was received several days ago would have answered it before now but have not had time until now. we have just moved into our new dwelling which is much more comfortable than the tents if it is covered with dirt. well Sallie we are under marching orders and it is very uncertain wether we will stay here or not but I am in hopes we will not have any hard marching to do this winter. Hope we will not have much of a winter as we will have to go on picket several times more before April and from the way Congress is acting we will have to on several times after April. Well it seems as if we are never to see any more pleasure at all and those who did not volenteer are to stay at home and enjoy themselves as though there was no war going on. well this is a hard world on some and easy on others. You know if I was President I would change things about and settle the goose question quick. my love to Callie tell her to write soon to me. Charly has joined an artillery Company that if they can make up one. Goodman is trying to make it up in Louisa Co. but I think it will be an uphill business. I have not joined yet but I will join that in preference to any other and especialy infantry for I am very tired of that. I dont know wether I shall join the Army next twelve months or not. except the sincere wishes of your affectionate

John Taylor Anderson

To Gordonsville
Camp Walker (Va) Feb 4 '62

Dear Sister

    With much pleasure I now seat myself to answer your welcome letter which was received last week. would have answered it before now but for going on picket we went on last last friday and came back last night. had quite a bad time if you remember it rained friday night and snowed all day Monday and we had no shelter, except what we could make of rails & brush you must know how we faired in such a condition as that. Well Sallie we have had dreadful weather ever since Christmas and no prospects of any better for some time yet. but hope we will have some good dry weather before long. We have no news at all now and nothing interesting going in except our capt has resined and gone home (Hope he will stay there) I dont know who will be elected in his place as the company is so split up in opinion but I should like Capt. Goodman if I could have my way about it but for this little time I dont care much how they do but they will have a lively time getting one into the company again. Well I dont know what to think about reinlisting. the Legislature dont seem to come to no conclusion about the raising the quota of Virginia and therefore I dont know wether to inlist or not but I will wait awhile before I will inlist at any rate would like to have some rest before I go for two years of the war which is some time off and right hard life at that but hope the war will end before that time and all will be peace and happiness but many lives may be lost before that time. well I must come to a close. Sallie this is late and I will stop so Goodbie

Yours affectionately
John Taylor Anderson

Camp Walker (Va)
Feb 18th 1862

Dear Sister

    Your interesting letter was received by me some day or two ago and with pleasure I perused its contents but was sorry to hear that the measles are again raging in that vicinity. Or Reg has just returned from picket; went on last Friday two cos were left to guard the regiment's property (cos. C & J were left) we have been on guard every other day since the Reg left I came off this eve at five o'clock and will have to go on tomorrow morning so you know I am sleepy as well as tired and fatigued did not sleep more than two hours last night so you can imagine how I feel to night at eight o'clock. I would not write at night but Richards is going home tomorrow and I will send it by him, Sallie they seem to be tarring us all to pieces down South but we heard that we had routed the enemy in Kentucky hope it is so but we heard to day that they had taken Fort Donalson and a great many of their guns, but dont believe this last report true, however the victory seems to be unknown that is who shal have it but hope we will be victorious, I will lieve the subject as well as I can not write any more I must close please write soon as I will be anxious to hear from the measles cases write all the news brought from Richmond

                Yours
                Affectionately
                John Taylor Anderson

To Gordonsville
May 2nd 1862
Camp at foot of Blue Ridge
mountain (VA)

Dearest Sallie

As Mr. Davis is going to Cville this morning I will write you a few lines. Ive left Standardsville last thursday about 12 o'clock and crossed the ridge before camping at all, we arrived here about 10 the following night, and very tired indeed We have been here ever since and no sign of amove in a day or two as I can see or hear. Jacksons forces are moving up the river on the other side that is they were the last time we heard from them. The Yankees are not very far from us just on the other side of the river; I dont know what their strenth is but I understand that there is two divisions. dont know wether it is so or not; the day we crossed the ridge was very cloudy and it was quit a novel sight to waid through the clouds. they divuged the mountains and it was so thick you could not see a person fifty steps. Well Sallie I expect to have a hard time of it this summer I should not be surprised if we never got to another camp that is a place where we will stay any time. we have been moving ever since we left Manassa & will never stop until next winter and you know we must have a hard time and worse now than ever because we have gotten so far from the railroad & have all the provisions to hall with wagons. we have not had anything since yesterday and I dont see any chance for any today. the wagons have gone back to Gordonsville after them but they cannot get here before tomorrow morning if they travel all night; well I am getting pretty tired of living this way but see no chance for a change, I should like to have the priviledge of going home just for a short time; I feel badly have been feeling so for some time and cannot get anything fitting to eat, we have no flower or anything fitting to make bread. if you can I wish you would send me some if you can get it.

I understand Mr Parrot has a plenty of it. if Mr. H concludes to send us Phill you can send it by him. I have not heard a word from you since I left you. I find my boots are two heavy for summer i will try and get Mr Davis to carry them to Cville if he will, and some of you can get them from there but I dont recon he will carry them. well I must close. my love to all and except the kindess wishes of your brother

Taylor Anderson

Please send me a pack of invelops if you can get them & find a chance to send them

Goodbye Taylor

~

To Gordonsville   Camp at foot of Blue Ridge (Va)
                         May 1862

Dear Sister
    As I have a chance to send a letter to Cville, I will drop you a few lines to let you where I am. we had quite a long march yesterday. I feel better than anyone might expect though I am quite bilbous yet but will try and keep up. We expect to meet Jackson tomorrow. well as the drum has beatin I must stop

Goodbie
Taylor Anderson

Sallie F Anderson
Gordonsville Orange Co Va
Augusta Co June 12th 1862

Dearest Sallie

It has been a long time since I heard from you and how often have I wished that I could read one more of your letters but that sweet priviledge has been denied me and I am afraid it will be a long time before I can hear from you again. I trust you will not forget to pray for me I have God I put my trust in him for I feel that he alone can protect me and save me from such pestilence as we have in our land. Sister trust that you will often pray for me and never forget me when you kneel to pour forth your thanks to God for his kind protection over you and your relations and it is my prayer that he will protect you. I often think of the pleasant hours we have spent together and feel now that we may never be blessed again. I have no hopes of peace while I see nothing or no prospects of anything but war, and while that lasts we must be subjected to the consequences of such a war and they are very severe especially in this part of the world, we never stay twenty four hours in one place and very often march all day & night without eating or sleeping, at one time we marched two hundred and thirty miles in ten days & stood on the battlefield three days out of that ten, our Reg was engaged last Sunday near the Union church about halfway between Harrisonburg and Port Republic. the fight lasted about six hours we were not engaged until about three O'clock in the eve, when we were marched up under perfect range of one of their battries for about one mile and they raked us with shell and canaster shop from four of their guns. we were ordered not to fire untill we get about two hundred yards of their batery, when we were ordered to fire. we poured it into them but they certainly did rake us bad with their guns, men fell on my right and left, but I were spared, between

103

forty & fifty were wounded in our regiment and two were killed. Parrish of our co. killed, Melton, one hundred mortally wounded died yesterday. Lewis Robertson slightly wounded while we were at Winchester. I lost my knapsack and every rag of clothes I had. I borrowed a dirty shirt to day and washed it and put it on. it is only clean one I have had for four weeks. I wrote to Carter to get me some hose. I wish you would get some one to see Sam Atkins & get those shirts from him if he has not sent them and send me as many pairs of socks as you can. start I prefer your socks if you can get them out to me some way please be in a hurry so Andrew will have chance to get to me before we move off again. Thom Lancaster was certainly taken by the Yankees. I havent seen him as we left him below Charlestown which was fed & I have not heard from him since. please write if you have a chance. my love to Pa. tell him to remember an abscent boy in his prayers.

I heard Mr. H was sick my love to him my love to all. remember me to their God

Taylor Anderson

I sent some money to Carter if you or Puss need any you can ask it from him.

July 10 1862

Dear Sister

After a long and tiresome journey I have goten with my Reg but did not get with it until this morning. I left Richmond thursday evening walked untill late that night and yesterday all day untill midnight last night and when I found them they were about six miles from R coming on back. we are at this time on the Central road about two miles above Richmond but how long we will stay here is unknown but I am inclined to think that we will stay here several days. Tell Dick I can not find jimmie he is not with the Regt or has not been with it since we left him at the hospital. all of our men have been sent from that hospital and I am in hopes jimmie has goten off home before this time. I cannot hear anything from him atall and if he has not goten home I dont know wether to advise dick to come to look for him or not. recon he would find him. I cannot tell. well Sallie I spent some of the most unhappy hours yesterday I ever spent in my life I cannot tell what, but I were miserable all day. well I must close you must write soon my love to all & tell them to remember me in their prayers.

PS This paper received a pretty severe wound in the thursday battle. Tell Miss Jennie my flowers have withered my love to her

Taylor

I have goten my shirts from Mr. Mason

Taylor Anderson

Letters of James C. Ogg

(Relative of J.T. Anderson)

Private, Co. C, 13th Virginia Infantry
(Gordonsville Grays)

Pegram's Brigade
Early's Division
Army of the Shenandoah

Smith's Brigade
Early's Division
Army of Northern Virginia

Fairfax Station (Va)
Aug 19th 1861

Miss Sallie

Dear Friend I Avail myself of this Opportunity to write you a few lines. the wether is cloudy and rainy and Everything looks so lonely that my whole injoyment is in communicating with my friends. Every one in camp are walking backwards and forewards from one place to another and look as if they do not know what to do with themselves. I think if some lady's wer in the neighborhood and we was allowed to go to se them we wouldn't feel so lonely I have not seen a respecful looking Lady since I have been here. when we wer over at winchester I could see some lady's Every day. all of the Repectable ladys in this vicinity had to leave when the Yankees caim thru here. I think there is more Amish in this Neighborhood than anything else. I hird a Catholik Priest Preach Sunday before last. the church is in the bounds of our camps. I liked everything better than his Dress. he had on and Od dress from anyone Else which I thought was unnessary. we have preaching very often in camp. John Jones from Louisa courthouse Preaches for us nearly Every Sunday at an Episcopal Church In the range of our camp and a young man from Hampshire City Va Preaches for us very often. we also have prayer meetings very often in camp. Sally you must not think of me for not writeing to yu before this. I have but little time to write Excepting Being within when we cannot drill. Saly I hird today the Yankee calvary surrounded 6 of our pickets and I supposed they took them Priseners. they have not be hird from since. two of the Pickets caim in camp last night. they sayed they did not know where the others wir. the Yankey Caliry was sayed to be 100 in number while our Pickets was only 8 in number. The Yankeys may be advancing on us. it is common for them to drive the pickets in before they make an attack on the main body of the army. Well Saly I hird that Moly and Charles Louis wir going to be married and you and James Knanforer. I hope you all will wait until I get back and invite me to your wedings. It would afford me a great deal of pleasure to be at your wedings and yours especially. It would afford me the greatest of pleasure to be at yours. I had rather get a letter from my absent friends than to eat a meal of Vitules after fasting 2 days I hope you will not feel any delicasy in writing to me for your memory is very dear to me though far in away I very frequently think of you when at church, the ladys wir very kind to us in winchester. the best water I ever drank I thought was on the other side of the Blueridge. On our way to Manasus Junction I was very thirsty & stopped at a house and a lady gave me as much water as I wanted and filled my canteen Please answer this by doing so you will oblig your friend so good by for this time

As ever your friend
James C. Ogg

PS Please pass this letter Direct your letters to Fairfax station 13 Reg Va Volinteers

(James Ogg—son of Samuel Ogg of Louisa, Virginia)

(Sallie's sisters married his brothers.)

Camp Blair (Va) Sept 19th 1861

My Dear Friend

I received your kind letter of the 30 in due time & was glad to hear from you but sorry to hear that you was sick. I have neglected answering your letter the Reason is I have been on the March nearly ever since to and from Falls Church. The last time I was in a skirmish we had 300 of our Regiment..& 2 pieces of the Washington Artillery..and 100 of Col. Stewards Cavalry. we attacted a briggade of the Yankeys at Lewinsville and run them off without losing a man. we took 4 prisoners. John and Charles were with us. They are both well at this time & held out very well on the march. Some 10 of our boys went out skirmishing below Munsons Hill last thursday in which David Mcgruter received a wound which I fear will prove fatal to him tho the Doctor says their are very good chances for him to get well. he is at Falls Church at this time too sick to be moved.

Lieutenant Goodman arrived here last evening. he looks badly yet a good many of our boys are sick with the fever and colds. Sally you sayed I seemed anitious to see you off. I cant think why you should think so. I certainly hird you was going to be married. Far from my wanting to get you off. I asure you that you are not incommoding any one so far as I am concerned. I hope you do not think so.

You must not think hard of me for writeing short letter. my pen is so bad I am afraid you wont be able to read what I have writen.

Give my love to Molly when you se her and all of my friends in Louisa. this leaves me well. hoping it will find you and all well. write often. as ever your Fine friend with many good wishes for your welfare

J.C. Ogg
(Son of Samuel Ogg of Louisa, Va.)

Good by Sally

110

Dear Sallie

    I received your letter the other day & was glad to hear you was well again also to here that John had gotten home safe. I have no news that would interest you atall Except War news. I have a good deal of that, but nothing reliable. Expected to have to move from here several days ago. but have not yet. they are sending all the men off who are not fit for duty. Charles Carter started from here last Saturday for Manassus I hope they have sent him home. he was quite sick when he left here. I have not hird from him since. 10 of our men left the same day when Charles did. We have only 30 men here that is Privets. well Sallie I think it very Probible that we will have a fight before I will have a chance to write to you again. I think they are fixing for it at this time. President Davis was here last week. he stayed several days at the courthouse. We saluted him with cannon when he past here also musketry. you will pleas Excuse bad writing as my pen is very bad I must close. write often. I remain your friend JCO

Goodbye Sallie

(James C. Ogg was the brother of Richard and Andrew Ogg who married Sallie's sisters.)

To Miss Sallie f Anderson
Gordonville Va

May 25th 1862,
Chapins Bluff (Va)

Miss Sallie

As I have not heard from you for some time I will write you a few lines to let you heare from me. this leaves me well. I enjoy better health Since the Spring set in. We are now about 8 miles below Richmond on the river near the front. We are tolerbly well Quartered in the shed of a barn. plenty of straw to lie on. go on pickett. Some times get half rations. I suppose you have heard of the fight when the gun boats came up. We crossing the River at the time but was not fired on. the front is on the South Side of the river. We are on the North side. We are making a mass batry on this side. They can never pass this place unless they attack the batirrys by land and take them but each batterry is so constructed as to protect Each other. Johnson attacted the enemy on frida Evening and repulsed them. I do not know with what loss. thay renewed the fight again yesterday morning. thay kept up a heavy cannonading all day. have not heard from them. there are no line of the gun boats coming up now. we are reddy for them whin they come. We have a bludy battle before us. Thay will make a Desparate effort to take Richmond. this is a fine country down heare. I have no more news to write my best respects to you and friends. pleas write soon and let me hearew from you. from your friend Jos. F Bibb

Direct your letter Richmond Va Co C 56 Regi. Va Voluns

J.F. Bibb

To Miss Sallie F Anderson Gordonsville

Camp near Richmond
June 21st 62

Miss Sallie

We are tolerably well quartered in tents and about 2 miles from Richmond and have resumed the old order of things. we have our company Drill and battalion Drill every day—I am well sitting in a butiful grove that is so pleasant. Oh it wold be a pleasure to one to sit in such a butiful place if it was not for the madness of the two contending parties which keep this unholy war in progress killing the very best blud of this once happy people.

I hope through the goodness of God once again to behold those many kind faces of relations and friends it wold be one thing but impossible for us to have a furlough When our twelve months expire. I understand that Jackson is on his way here. if so we will have a fight heare in a few days if not sooner. I am sure these and a great many soldiers arrived heare last night got heare yesterday from Georgia. will at a assuredly fight when they attempt to take Richmond. This leaves me well and hope it may find you the same remember my respects to Miss Mollie and tell cos Callie Richard and Cos Nannie and my best love to you Miss Sallie. if it be not pleasing to much of you write to me immediately on the reception of this. You can hardly imagine the pleasure it gives me to heare from you. give me all the news both good and bad. Believe me your friend as ever

Jos F Bibb

June 1st 1862
Camp on Blackwater (River Va)

Miss Sallie F Anderson

Cousin Sallie

I now take my seat to write you a few lines to let you all know how I am getting along. Cousin Sallie I am getting as fat as a pig. My regt is still on Blackwater. The Yankees paid us one visit since we came back from Suffolk their forces were estimated at from ten to fifteen thousand. my regt went over the River on friday and drove in their pickets. I said the regt it was not but seven companys and two pieces of artillery. On Saturday the second and eleventh Miss went down about four miles from the river and had a skirmish with the yankees. There was three companys of my regt thrown out as skirmishers. My company was one of the companies I was not with the company I volunteered to go in front of the skirmishers and find out where the yankees were stationed at. We deployed as skirmishers which threw me in the road; I had to go down the road all of the way and the yankees firing on us for half a mile there was from five to fourteen yankees firing on me all of the time. We charged them and made them skedadle. They did not start to run until we got with in a hundred and fifty yards of them. They fell back about one hundred yards and stopped to give us another fight. We charged up within fifty yards of them again before they started to run again. I fired six shots within fifty yards of them. I killed one yankee 20 yards of me. There was seven in rthe squad and when I killed this one the other six shot at me but did not touch me. one ball passed my foot about two inches It is a wonder they had not of killed me. I reckon you are tired or reading my description of the skirmish. I will only be getting me two good yankee haversacks and three canteens and a bedroll of blankets india rubber cloth and came

118

back to camp. We got back to camp at one o'clock in the night. Cousin Sallie your friend Jim Norford is in our brigade now Capt Steardivants battery is in our brigade above us on the river the yankees have gone back to Suffork after tearing up the Petersburg and Norfolk Rail Road and taking the iron to Suffolk. Everything looks disheartening in Miss from what I hear. There is a rumor in camp of being mounted and going to Miss but I do not want to go to Miss. I had much rather stay here in Virginia until the war ends. I would like to be mounted but I do not want to go to Miss. If I liv to see next winter I am going to reenlist in some calvary company if I can. I have as good health as I have ever had in my life. I guess you all were very badly scared when you heard that the yankees were at Louisa Court House. I was very uneasy myself for fear they might come to Gordonsville. I heard once that they were in Gordonsville but then I heard it contradicted. Cousin Sallie I must bring my letter to a close as I guess you are getting tired of reading my nonesense. give my respects to all the neighbors that I know and give my love to Aunt Sarah & the children & Uncle Jessie & Uncle Charles. I must close by saying write soon to your friend Jimmie L Lewis. Direct your letters to Franklin Va Co D 2nd Regt Miss Inf in care of Capt Brandon

119

Letter of Nicholas Johnson

Private, Co. E, 13th Virginia Infantry

Culpeper Riflemen
Fourth Brigade
Johnston's Division
Army of the Shenandoah

Brandy Rifles

The following letter of Private Johnson to his sister, Mrs. B.R. Fox of Louisa Courthouse, Virginia, gives his eyewitness account of action on the battlefield at First Manassas.

Dear Sister

I expect you are very uneasy about us up here as you have heard nothing from us since the great battle of Manassas junction. We happened not to get there in time for the fight but came very near it and would have been but for a collision on the Manassas road. The fight commenced at four o'clock Sunday morning and we got there about four in the evening and hurried out to the battle field with the full expectation of fighting but when we got there we found the enemy under full flight and our men pursueing them. We took a great many prisoners and a great deal of baggage consisting of knapsacks and clothes of various kinds. We took also about 200 horses and wagons of the best kind and a great deal of artillery I suppose the value of the property all together would amount to over $300,000. I wish I had time and paper to give you a full description of the fight but you can see from this scrap how scarce it is. None of our boys have any paper so I do not know when you will hear from me again. We are now out here about 10 miles from the junction and 12 from Alexandria and two from Fairfax C.H. I am unable to say where we are going I rather think that we are on our way to take Alexandria or the Arlington heights and it will be a very bloody battle. I do not know what our loss was at the battle of Manassas though it was very heavy on both sides I went the next morning over a portion of the battle filed and I think I saw 250 dead or wounded and I don't think that was a fourth of the number. You need not send me any more boxes as we can not get them. Tell Annie that I got her letter and will answer as soon as I get some paper. Love to all and write soon. Your bro. Tipp;

Direct your letters to Manassas.

J

Letters and Items Pertaining to Sergeant William C. Kiblinger

Co. I, 10th Virginia Infantry

Stewart's Brigade
Ewell's Corps
Army of Northern Virginia

Through the courtesy of William H. Kiblinger of Mineral, Virginia, the letters and other items pertaining to his grandfather, Sergeant William C. Kiblinger of Conrad's Store, Rockingham County, Virginia, are presented here:

(1)   Letters to his wife Elizabeth

(2)   Letter to his brother John N. Kiblinger of Washington College, Tennessee

(3)   Letter of Captain S.A. Sellers regarding a furlough

(4)   Copy of indorsements of approval of a furlough that had to be approved at company, regimental, brigade, and corps levels and finally by Gen. R.E. Lee's Army Headquarters

(5)   Copy of Hd Qrs Army of the Potomac Special Orders No. 354 granting a disability furlough

(6)   U.S. Army letter issued at Appomattox Courthouse, Virginia, to Sergeant Kiblinger as a paroled prisoner of war

(7)   Amnesty Oath signed by William Kiblinger at the Office of the Provost Marshal, U.S. Army, at Harrisonburg, Virginia, 15 June 1865

Camp near Gordonsville
June 22, 1862

My Dear & affectionate wife, (Elizabeth)

I wrote a letter to send by Dr. Miller but he will not come over so will send them by John Huffman. I send you three cherry seeds. They are a very large grey cherry. They are very nice and I wish you would plant them for yourself & me. We are still (at) Gordonsville but I expect we will leave on the train tonight or in the morning. The troops are all going toward Richmond. But I must quit. If you have not got my satchell yet you had better send for it or else them clothes will rot. But adieu for the present. I will come home as soon as I can so trust in God & all will be well with us for he is a rewarder of them that diligently seek him.

If we go down the Richmond road I will pass within fifty feet of where my sister lives. I would like to stop & see her but I do not expect I will have time. But adieu for the present. I am well & hope this may fine you enjoying good health, and Tyree & the rest of the family also. My best love to you and may God bless & protect and save you & Tyree from all harm & danger.

Pray for your much erring husband & for peace in our country.

Write the first opportunity.

Your affectionate husband,
Wm. C. Kiblinger

March 8, 1863
Camp Snickers Neck (Va.)

Dear Brother, (John Q.N. Kiblinger)

I seat myself to drop you a few lines this beautiful Monday morning as it has been some time since you have heard from me. You would like to have the past history of my past service. I will give it to the best of my recollection Our Company left home for Harpers Ferry the 18th of April 1861. We got there on Sunday morning. The arsenel had been burned there. We had a very good time there except we had to drill very hard, (we had a splendid Colonel, his name was

S.B. Gibbon. He was a very nice and good man. He was kind to his men. His name will be handed down to generations yet unborn) but I believe I am digressing. But excuse me for when I speak of our Colonel it awakes sad recollections. We stayed at the ferry some months. We did not have much discipline there. We came up to Winchester from there and stayed there a day or two then we marched out to Romney some 40 or 50 miles to meet the enemy but when we got there they had left. There was a detachment sent after them which over taken them and taken one piece of artillery and burned the railroad bridge a few miles from Romney. We stayed here several days and then marched back to Winchester. There was a force of Yankees a coming up from Martins (Martinsburg). We then March out to meet them. We went down as far as Darksville and offered fight to the enemy four days. We were down there on the 4th of July. It was ascertained that the enemy would not advance we had orders to leave there. It went mightely against the men to retreat from there. They called the General a coward for not advancing instead of retreating. We did not know very much about it (then) as now. We were all keen to get into a fight. We had not been in one yet. We came back to Winchester and then we had orders to leave for Manassas. We got there on the 21st. When we got off the cars the cannon were booming in the distance. We were ordered to leave napsacks & haversacks and march to the field of battle. We double quicked for six miles. The dust was shoe mouth deep. You could not see your file leader the dust was flying so. When we got to the field a courier met us and told (us) to forward for our General was in the front of the battle.

We now get on the field. We hear the roar of musketery. Now we meet the wounded a coming out. Oh horrible sight. Some tell us we are whipped but we now meet some of the New Orleans Tigers, they tell us that "the ball is open, there is plenty of room to dance." They tell us the enemy is giving way . . . a few more minutes will give us the victory. We go a piece further and form a line of battle (the enemy was trying to flank us) The enemy advance on our right wing. Our right wing gave them a volley and they retreat. Our batteries had been playing on the enemy all the time.

The enemy retreats at our advance. I only fired one shot in this fight. We came back to the Junction that night. We only eat once that day. We were too tired to cook any that night. The next day (Monday) it rained all day but we went below the Junction this evening and camped. Next day (Tuesday) Started for Fairfax Station, got there some time in the night, no cooking, got hardbread which we took from the Yankees. We fell back to Centerville. Stayed there for some time and then we left there and fell back within three miles of Manassas and put up winter quarters. Here we stayed until the 9th of March and Johnston then our General fell back from there on the south side of the Rappahannock river, there we heard so much about General Jackson in the Valley and that Jackson was giving back and the Yankees were coming up the Valley. The men of the Regt get dissatisfied . . . want to go to Jackson. Will not reenlist. A great many ran off and went home. Our Colonel (God bless . . . I hope he is in Heaven) went to Richmond and got us transferred to Jackson. The Lt. Col. came and told us. You ought to have heard the shout which ascended up from that wicked crowd. We take up our line of march for Rockingham. After a day or so of march it commenced raining and rained for several days. We got to Stanardsville and stayed all night. We were treated first rate there by the citizens. We had houses to stay in. We were fixed up in fine style, plenty to eat free of charge. The Col said we would stay there provided the men wouldn't get drunk, but some of them could not stand it. They had to drink and we had to leave so we went up to Walkers and the Regt stayed in the barn but I struck for home. Went to the top of the mountain that night and stopped. Next morning I started for home, got there a while after dinner. Jackson was then at Elk Run Church. Stayed at home 3 or four days then (Jackson pulled up stakes and after Millroy he put) we went up past Port Republic, crossed the mountain at Brown's Gap. We went by Mechams Station.

Some of the troop taken the cars there. Our Regt. went on to the first station this side of the tunnel, there we taken the cars that night for Staunton. We got there in the morning. We went to the blind assilum to get breakfast but we did not get it. The wagons came up and our Col. was dissatisfied about not getting breakfast for us. (So we did not get anything to eat there). We could not buy a loaf of bread, but they had been soldiers before. So we marched some three or four miles from town then such cooking. We stayed here a couple of days then after Millroy we put. We overhauled him on the eighth of May. Oh! sadest day here we lost our Col. whose superior is not in the Southern Army.

Spotsylvania County (Va.)
May 7th 1863

My dear and affectionate wife, (Elizabeth)

I seat myself to drop you a few lines this evening. We had a fight with the enemy on the second of May . . . fought them Saturday evening and Sunday. We had hard fighting on Sunday. Our Regt suffered very much. We had 3 killed James Phillips, Charlie and Elant Wyant and Philip Secrist wounded and Peter Sellers and Bob Harsberger, Noah Frayzies and Joe Monger, Dan Secrist and Capt. Sam Sellers and Geo Miller were taken prisoner. We have drove the enemy across the Rappahannock river. Oh my beloved I am still unharmed through the goodness and mercy of God which I am very thankful for. Oh we should raise our hearts in thankfulness to God for his goodness to us. Oh my beloved wife thank him for sparing your husband through the conflict & ask him to be with him in future to guide & direct him at all time. But I must change my subject.

The enemy crossed the river yesterday. They threw their baggage in every direction. The victory was complete, I think. I hope it will close the war. But I want to write a few lines to sister (Louisa Kiblinger Porter). It is late in the evening so I will have to close. I am well except a cold. But hope these few lines may find you & Tyree enjoying good health. May God bless & protect & shield you from all harm & danger is the prayer of your much erring husband. Adieu, God bless you.

Your affectionate husband,
Wm. C. Kiblinger

To all whom it may concern . . .

The bearer herewith Wm. C. Kiblinger, a private of Captain S.A. Sellers Company "I" 10th Regt Va Infty aged 32 years, 5 feet 7 inches high, florid complection, gray eyes, dark hair and when enlisted, a blacksmith, born in the county of Rockingham, State of Virginia and enlisted at Conrads Store, Rockingham Co., Va. on the 18th day of April 1861 to serve one year, is hereby permitted to go to his home in Rockingham County Va., he having received a furlough from the ninth day of January 1864 to the twenty-third day of

January 1864 at which time he will rejoin his company or Regt wherever it may then be or be considered a deserter. Subsistance has been furnished to said Wm. C. Kiblinger to the ninth day of January 1864 and pay to the first day of November of 1864.

Given under my hand at camp near Rapidan this the 9th day of Jany 1864.

S.A. Sellers
Capt Co. "I", 10th Va. Inf.

Private Wm. C. Kiblinger has never had a furlough, has never been absent without leave and has been when well enough for duty in all battles in which the Regt has been engaged. He has been a faithful soldier and has a wife and children dependent upon him.

S.A. Sellers
Capt. Co. "I" 10th Va. Infty

William Carpenter Kiblinger
1831-1908

Office Provost Marshal,

Harrisonburg, Va., June 15 1865.

AMNESTY OATH.

I, _William Kiblinger_ of _Rockingham_ county, Virginia, do solemnly swear, in the presence of ALMIGHTY GOD, that I will henceforth faithfully support, protect, and defend the Constitution of the United States, and the UNION of the States thereunder, and that I will, in like manner, abide by and faithfully support all laws and proclamations which have been made during the existing rebellion reference to the emancipation of slaves, so HELP ME GOD.

[SIGNED] _W. C. Kiblinger_

Sworn to, and subscribed before me

this _15_ day of _June_ 1865. _M. J. White_ Prov. Marshal.

I certify on honor that the above is a true copy. _M. J. White_ Provost Mar.

Appomattox C.H. Va
April 10th 1865

The Bearer Sergeant M. C. Kislinger Co. "B"
10th Va Infantry a paroled prisoner of the
Army of Northern Virginia has permission to
go to his home and there remain undisturbed

Wm Lee Martz
Lt Col Comdg Regt

Letters of Private James O. Chisholm

Captain Wiley G. Coleman's Company
Virginia Heavy Artillery

F.W. Smith's Battery
(Third Richmond Howitzers)
Reserve Artillery
Second Corps,
Army of Northern Virginia

The following letters of Private James Chisholm from Hanover County, Virginia, to his sister, Anna Marie, include his account of an execution of several soldirs and his hope for promotion to Corporal so he could get a horse to ride in his artillery unit.

Centreville (Va.)
Oct. 17th 1861

Dear Sister

As I am at liesure this morning I will write you a few lines to inform you that we are all well and hope that you all are enjoying the same blessing. We started from Richmond last Thursday and we have had a very tedious time since we did not get to Manassas until last Saturday morning, it took us all day to fix our tents & Sunday morning we had to work all day packing up our annunition & on Monday morning we struck tents and took up a line of march for Fairfax Court House, and that night an alarm was beat about 3 o'clock. The roll was called and everything put in readiness but it proved to be false. The pickets guards on Tuesday morning had a little fight. Did not any of our men get killed but we took one Yankee prisoner at one o'clock last Tuesday night the whole army had to retreat back to Centreville six miles or so of Manassas, all of them had to burn everything they could not carry. At Fairfax C.H. they burned forty or fifty barrels of flour & at our company I saw with my own eyes, bags of corn, hey & they had even to burn some of their tents, camp stools, cots, trunks and every little thing of that kind. Some of our men rather than to see them burnt up took some of the tents and brought them on our cannon. I got about 50 yrds. of new white cloth and brought along with me. I take it and spread it down in the bottom of our tent to lie on. We expect a fight every day no one can tell when it will come off. We may here to be in the fight. if we do I trust in God that we all may come out safe.

The men in our company did not seem like they were at all afraid. We are now in about 7 miles of the enemy. The retreat was made from Fairfax to try and draw the Yankees out if we can get them on the same old battlefield. I think it will be the last battle they will fight in a long time. We are certainly well fixed. We have two hundred thousand fighting men ready to meet them any day they may chose to come. We have two or three hundred pieces of artillery.

Capt. Coleman's nephew has gotten a transfer into our company. He is from Missippi. You all must not give yourselves any uneasiness on our account for we are getting on very well. I will be a splendid cook and washer. I think if I stay up here we have to do all of our own washing, etc. I sent you my likeness before I left Richmond by Mr. John. If we stay here awhile near Christmas I and Billy will try and get a furlough. We will be near the first that will get any, for we have never had one yet. As I am tired of writing I will close. Give my love to Pa and all the family and except a portion for yourself.

I remain your affectionate
Brother until death
J.O.C.

P.S.

You must excuse bad writing & spelling and all mistakes.
Direct your letter to Manassas Junction to the care of
Capt. Coleman under Colonel Pendleton

Centreville (Va.)
Dec. 15th 1861

Dear Sister,

I received your letter last Monday and was glad to hear that you were well. This leaves us both tolerably well at present, except colds.

I should have written yesterday but was prevented we were busy busy, trying to finish our winter quarters. We will get them done by next Tuesday if nothing happens. We expect to move into them the last of the week. It will be quite a little town up here, about a hundred houses in all. I have no news to write of this time everything is pretty still up here. I don't think there is any danger of our having another fight here. I don't believe the Yankees are ever coming any more. Last Monday two men up here were shot for getting drunk and trying to pass the guards. They were tried by a Court martial and sentenced to be shot. They belong to the Tiger Rifles from New Orleans. Some of our company went over to see them shot, but I did not go myself.

We received a letter from home last Friday. They were all well. Albie wrote me word that you did not want me to carry the flag that it was too dangerous but I don't think there will be any more fighting so I will keep it while and see how I like it. If I don't like it very well I will let someone take my place. The Capt. says it is one of the most honorable posts in the army.

You wanted to know if I were coming down Christmas or not. I don't think there is any chance for any of us to come down before next February if we do this we have so many sick men. Out of our 89 men we have not more than fifty able for duty.

Write me word whether you have sold your turkeys or not and what you got for them. You may have them all. I want you to make me a pair of good thick pants and send them by the first opportunity. I have not got my boots yet but I have not needed them yet. I can do very well without them. I have a new pair shoes I have never had on which will last me a month or so I reckon.

I will close. Give my love to Aunt A. and Cousin Claris and all the family and except a large portion for yourself.

I remain your aff. Bro.
James O. Chisholm

Dear Sister,

I received your very welcome letter yesterday and was glad to hear from you. This leaves us all tolarably well at present and hoping when this reaches you it may find you all enjoying good health. I have not any news to communicate to you at this time everything is as quiet as can be. I don't hear any talk of a fight up here soon. I don't reckon there will be any fighting here before next spring. It is generally thought by the people that there will be a pretty large fight up here then. There is no chance for them to do anything this winter as the mud is so deep that the artillery can't be moved about. I was sorry to see in the papers our defeat in Kentucky. They may whip us out there but they will never do it here. We are so strongly fortified that one of our men could whip 8 Yankees. I heard some time ago that the Ashland Greys had enlisted for the war but I am in hopes it is not so for I want Alonzo S. Buck to come up here with us if they do have to come again. As I haven't any news to write I will close. Give my love to all the family and except a large portion for yourself.

I remain your aff. Bro.
J.O.C.

Camp Magruder Augt 25th 1864

Dear Sister

I write you a few lines to inform you that we are tolorably well at the present and hope that you all are enjoying the same health. We are now encamped at Sidney Church about three miles from Richmond I like very well myself, but Billy is very much dissatisfied he is getting home sick. We will stay where we are now for two or three months I hope, if not longer. We have got our horses & canon to get now. Capt Guys Company left this morning for the western part of Virginia They have been in service for three months We drill five times a day regually Our Company has determined on having Flying Artillery. I hope that I will get a Corporals place. If I do I will get a horse to ride All Artillery Companies have 8 Corporals. Capt Coleman has not appointed any of the officers yet We have 89 men. One of them was taken sick with the measles. It was a good thing we had it before we left home. We have got some very nice fellows in our Company. They are all divided off in messes of 16 All the nicest of them came in with us. We have hired a negro man to cook for us. We dont pay but 80 cts a piece a month for him. And I had much rather pay that than to be standing over a hot fire cooking. If you have not made my shirts you need not make them. I can get the cloth much cheaper here than you can in the country. I will have my likeness taken as soon as I get my uniform Which will be in a day or two. I would have written sooner but I had not the chance. Tell pa I will write to him next week if nothing happens. I stoodguard once since I have been down here. Billy was appointed Coprl for that day.

As I cannot think of writing any more I must clos. You must write as soon as you get this as I am particularly anxious to hear from home. Give my love to all enquiring friends and except a good portion for yourself.

Your Brother
J.O. Chisholm

P.S. Excuse bad writing & spelling
Direct your letter to Richmond care of Capt. Coleman

Letters
of
First
Lieutenant
Allen
Edens

of Marlboro County, South Carolina

Commander, Company E
4th South Carolina Cavalry
Butler's Brigade
Hampton's Division
Cavalry Corps
Army of Northern Virginia

The following is an extract from a letter to Lieutenant Edens' wife, Christian Chisholm of Clio, South Carolina, relating his experiences at the Battle of Trevilian Station, Louisa County, Virginia, 11-12 June 1864.

Bottoms Bridge,
Chickhomona River, Va
June 22, 1864

I have had a time—we have been on the tramp for 15 days—have fought 2 hard batles and had several skirmishes— we left Mechanicsville on Thursday morning the ninth of June and traveled two days and nights and attack the enemy Sat. morning at sunrise near Trevilian Station and had a severe batle lasting all day without decision on either side—the batle was renewed on Sunday at 3 oclock and raged with great fury until dark when the Yanks gave way and fled like wild goats leaving the ground strewed with dead and dying—our loss was heavy but not half that of the enemy—our Co. lost 1 killed, 1 severely wounded and 8 captured—Sunday we had 5 wounded making 15 for both days—loss of the Regt. about 90—Our whole loss will not exceed 600—that of the Yanks from 1500 to 2000—I fired all my pistol cartrages away—had three men wounded in the same jam of the fence by the balls—we was exposed to a galling fire both from cannon and small arms but God was our help in trouble.—one thing I know the Yankees was severely punished. —

The lieutenant was the maternal great, great grandfather of King McLaurin of St. Petersburg, Florida. The Florida native has five ancestors who fought in the battle and the story of his recent visit to the battlefield is contained in a newspaper article which appeared in the Central Virginian, *Louisa, Virginia, 10 September 1987.*

King McLaurin's great, great paternal grandfather Alex M. McLaurin was a trooper in the same company as was his great, great uncles Lauchlin A. McLaurin, James W. McLaurin, and Loch B. McLaurin, all of whom fought in the battle.

The following are excerpts from Lieut. Edens' letters to family members:

Raleigh, N.C. Mar. 23/1865

These lines will inform you that I am in good health and hoping that you are enjoying the same—I have been attending some horses which have been sent to the rear to recruit—I have sent you a mule to plow in place of the old mair—I hear that you have no horse to work and nothing to feed on—I am anxious to hear from home to know how the Yankees left you—do try to get me a letter soon—I have no money to send you yet as I have recd none in 10 months—you had better not plant more than 2 acres of cotton and that near the house.

Camp Middleton, S.C.
Mar. 24/64

We are under marching orders—where we will go I know not but it will be to Va. or the West—we are ordered to get rid of our baggage that is such as we cant cary on our horses—I will bon up several and send to Society Hill and you can get them from there—if we go to Va. we may come through that country—I hope you will be able to bear up under this trial and ever feel that we who put their trust in the Lord will be as Mount Sion which shall not be removed but abideth forever.

Danville, Va. May 19/64

I left Greensboro on the 14th and got to Danville on the 15th—Danville is a small town on the Dan River in Va. 4 or 5 mi. from the N.C. line—here we are detained by the tearing up of the RR of the Yankes—I cannot tell how long we shall be here—we have all ready been here 4 days and our horses are gon on and will very likely beat us to Richmond—I say us, I mean that part sent on by rail which is 110 men from the Regt.—there has been 3000 prisoners sent on to Georgia from this place since we got here and last night there was 200 Yankee Officers brought in—a great many of our wounded are also brought here—they all seem to be in good spirits—you have heard of the fighting in Va. and know more about it than I do for we get little news—we have heard that Capt. Thomas was killed and he is all the one from our district but I fear there is several more—that alone is a sad loss—I want to hear from you very mutch but do not expect a letter until I get to Richmond—if I ever do.— tell Ada and Hayne that I will write them as soon as I get to Richmond.

Richmond, Va./ May 23/64

I have just reached Richmond and in good health—I left Danville on Friday and met with the Regt. at Burkeville the same day then marched with the Regt. to this place—my horse has fallen away very mutch—so has all the horses—we are camping near where there was a batle last Wednesday— the ded horses are all around us—we shall move to the front in a day or two—the report is that Lee has fallen back—the Yankees have a very large force, so has Lee and there will be some fighting soon—there is no doubt but we shall be in a fight before you get this—times are hard here—corn meal is selling for 104 dollars per bushel, flower 500 dollars per bbl.—others upon a paralel—I have just got news our Gen. Waller has lost a leg and is a prisoner—we have lost many good men and will soon lose more—be very saving of bacon as it canot be got—tell the children to go to school regular—tell Hayne and Ada to write soon—I have a bad chance to write—I am still trying to be a Christian—Pray for me.

Miss Ada M. Edens,   Richmond   May 25/64

My Dear Daughter,

I have waited a long time to get a chance to write to you and I see no chance yet, but I will write you a few line today. I am well and hope you are the same. I have no news to write you. We expect to go to the front in a day or two. There is some fighting every day here and it is expected there will be another General engagement in a day or two. We have lost a great many men since the fighting began, but the Yankees have lost 4 or 5 to one. The Yankee Army is strong, but our Army is ready for them anytime. We have Forty Thousand Cavalry about Richmond. Ada, I am getting along as well as I expected. I hope that you will go to school all you can. I want you to get a good education. I want you to be careful how you conduct yourself. Modesty is the buty of women and above all get wisdom—that is that wisdom that cometh down from above. My advice is to go seek salvation. Do write to me and give me all the news and I will write a long letter to you next time. Give my kindness to all inquiring friends, if any. Nothing more at present so fair well.

Allen Edens

⁓

Bivac near Hanover C.H. Va.
May 29/1864

It is only through the mercy of God and the interposition of a kind providence that I am alowed to drop you these lines—yesterday we had a bloody fight—our Regt. went into the fight about 11 oclock and came out about 3 losing about one hundred and fifty men killed, wounded and missing—our Co. lost 13—Capt. Breeden wounded in leg—J.C. McRae shot thruogh body —H.H. Newton through knee—John Jones wounded and in hands of enemy—Ben Freeman the same— Charles Jackson missing—several others but not of your acquaintance —I was not hurt, though in perfect hailstorm of balls—three balls struck one small tree as I stood by it—we was outflanked and exposed to a terrific crossfire in this critical place—we lost many a noble man—we fought no doubt 20 to one—know not the loss of the enemy but it must have been heavy for they have fallen back this morning—we had by no means a fair showing—we had nothing engaged on our side but Cavalry, South Carolina and Va. but they fought like soldiers and died like men—there was two divisions of cavalry and two of infantry against us but we made the land too hot for them to advance on and we have any quantity of troops

here this morning and are all anxious for them to try again—
we expect a great batle in a day or two and no one is oneasy
about the result—I am well and my faithin God is strong—
Remember me in your prayers for this is a trying time.—I
have gone through the first batle safe and it an awful hot
one—men that have been in many batles say this was the
hardest of all.—The Lord be with you all and ma we all meat
again in time but if not when we shall part no more.

Savage Station, Va.   June 5/64

There has been another great batle since I wriot you but
I was not in that—The Yankees was defeated with great
loss—they lost 10 to 1—they have been defeated in every
fight and I pray God it may continue so—they are still moving and there will be another batle soon. We are nearly broak
down—We have been marching and fighting for 10 days with
hardly time to eat—I am better satisfied than I expected to
be but I am tired of war—some think it will end soon but
it will not end as long as the Yankees can find a man to
fight.—We have a powerful army here now and that cannot
be conquered.—Please remember me to the children—keep
them going to school—tell Mag to write me also Ada and
Hayne.

Stony Creek, Va.   June 29/64

On Friday fighting at Hopewell Church.—We drove the enemy several miles killing many and capturing over 100 prisoners last night.—Our Brigade was in it again later. I was not with it—this is the first fight I've mssed—I was too unwell to go but they gave the Yankees fits so it is all rite but I always like to have a part in the game.—We are faring well for rations, get plenty of meat and bread and some coffee and sugar—horses fair bad—my horse played out or nearly so. The Yankees are shelling Peters Beling today—nearly all of both armies are on south side of James River—a great many sick men—you must not think me very sick—have slight diaree—I hope to be well soon as officers are scarce.—Tell Hayne I want to see him soon and the same regard to Ada. Tell Mag and Willy, Drady, Frances and Jo howdy and to be good children—I want to see my baby, Allen, some of the worst.—I hope he will be a good boy and give Miss Mary R as little trouble as possible.

Greensboro, N.C.
March or Early April 1865

I received your letter while lying behind a hastily built breastworks waiting the approach of the enemy but he did not come—we do not suffer for food, we suffer sometimes for time to draw and cook but we are willing to suffer if we can drive these miserable vandals from the land for they are worse than you ever herd they was—they take everthing in their reach even from poor women and they even take the last thing they have to live on, shot down the last milk cow in the yard and butcher it and cary it off saying that is the only way they can whip us—I have been 5 days without taking off my saddle but once and have not had off my boots but one night in 15 days but all that I am willing to endure—we are in fine spirits.

Bivwac near Stony Branch Station, Va.   July 12/64

I am in better health today than I have been for several days—I have no news to write—we have several sick men but none have died with disease out of our Co.—we have lost 31 killed—the wounded are dying very fast in Richmond—they have what is called gangrene which rots out the flesh—many of our Regt. have died from wounds—we shall all be afoot—our horses got no corn for several days at a time—My horse no doubt is dead. I rode him down and sent him to the recruiting camp—There instead of recruiting them they perish them to death—I am very mutch displeased for I have thought so mutch of that horse—you never saw such horses as ours are—in fact one half of them are already dead—as for ourselves we get plenty to eat—I had a severe spell of toothache last night but feel better today.

I have red of war and heard of war but this reality is an awful thing passed description.—The firing commences slowly in front, the command is forward and soon we meet the ambulance corps bearing the wounded and dying to the rear.—the firing now encreases to a steady roar which is kept up until one cide or the other is compelled to give way—At this moment the victorious dash forward with a yell and the

149

batlefield unvails its awful face—the young man upon whos rosy cheeks 18 sumer suns has shone lies coald and still upon the ground—again I see the man in the very viger and strength of manhood bathing in his own hearts blood—but is that all?—no, no behold the man of riper years who has found all the associations of life as he lies prostrate on the ground his life slowly ebing out drop by drop—he meets his fate as becomes a man, but there is one thing that seems to bear heavily on his mind 'Oh my dear wife and little ones at home who will care for them now', but as the messenger draws near the news is boarn from on high, 'I will be a father to the fatherless and a companion to the widow', the spirit takes its flight and the body is comited to the soldiers shallow grave on the batlefield and awaits the summons to meat the Lord in the sky.—It is sadening to think of all the bloody carnage that is abroad in our once peaceful land, our dear sunny South.—I have just been looking out at the lovliness of this beautiful night and wondering what dark scens the palefaced Queen of night is calmly looking upon—alas, upon how many sticken hearts the silvery moon unheeded sheds her soft rays tonight.—Rays rest upon the home of the lighthearted and gay and at the same time they glimer over the graves of the brave and trew who are sleeping far from their loved ones in a strange land. May they rest in peace.—Ive been thinking and comparing the present with the past and the natural conclusion is that I am filled with sad thoughts and feelings and sorrow for those whom this cruel war has made widows and fatherless—, oh, hasten the day when peace shall be proclaimed.

In January 1865 Lieutenant Edens' company was transferred to Columbia, South Carolina, to oppose Union General William T. Sherman's forces. His eldest child, Hayne, age 16, enlisted in March 1865 and was killed the same month. The men in the company did not surrender. The troopers disbanded and rode home on April 20, 1865, from Hillsboro, North Carolina.

Letter
of
George
Hill
Winfrey

Private
Company D
  Buckingham Yancey Guards
  Buckingham County, Virginia
  56th Virginia Infantry
  Hunton's Brigade
  Pickett's Division
  First Army Corps
  Army of Northern Virginia

The following letter of George Hill Winfrey was written to his son, Joseph Winfrey, M.D., of Glen Allen, Virginia. This memoir depicts in vivid terms the most trying and harrowing events and circumstances surrounding his family and their efforts to survive the hardships brought on by the war. Of particular interest is the ingenuity displayed by the hard pressed people of the South, who by indefatigable persistence and fortitude, managed to eke out a scant livelihood during this period of national crisis.

This way of life was typical of most families throughout the impoverished South.

George Winfrey was severely wounded in his right shoulder at the Battle of Cold Harbor but returned to duty following his recuperation.

Milburn — Apr. 1, 1903

My dear Joseph,

Yours of 27th ult. to hand, I would take pleasure in writing out for you the reminiscences you ask for, — but for the stiff and palsied condition of my fingers, which renders writing, — in a legible manner, very tedious and laborious to me, I hope you will be able to decipher what I may write.

Would that I could depict those trying times, in a more lucid manner, — in such a style as to make on your mind, a *picture* of the trying, — harrowing events and circumstances which environed us, particularly the dear ones at home, while husbands, fathers, and sons were away, on the tented plain, or on the gory field, — shedding their lifes blood, to repel the ruthless invaders, — descendants of the same *canting*, hypocritical "Roundhead Puritans (?)" who rebelled against, dethroned, and deliberately put to death their rightful sovereign, creatures who, during all the intervening time, had lost none of their traits transmitted to them by their regicidal ancestors, — except indeed their invincible *courage*, thus leaving them, — of course with some individual exceptions — without one noble or redeeming trait, — creatures, whose diabolical hatred of the South, was, and *is*, exceeded *only* by their Contemptible All consuming love of the Allmighty Dollar. Before I proceed further, let me set you right on your nomenclature. In your allusion to the war, you call it the *Civil War*, — You make me tired. I know nothing of any war of *rebelion*, — nor any civil war in this country, since the days of the Revolution. A Civil war is a war between citizens of the same state, or between two parties each owing and acknowledging allegiance to the same General Head, — or government, — but differing as to which party shall have general control and direction of that government, — The Hon. Henry A. Wise ex governor of *Va* advocated war for our rights *within* the Union. Had his advice been followed, *then* it would have been a *"Civil war"* — a war between two parties under the same general government, each seeking by force of arms, to direct and control its policiy.

But this you know was not the nature of the war between the States, By secession, the Southern States, simply renounced their *Statehood*, and by that act renounced all claims to the protection of the Federal government of any right to direct and control its affairs, — asking or claiming of it no more than of England or France, or any other *Foreign* Government. When you allude to the war, — please have regard for correct nomenclature, — loyally to your old Mother Virginia, *respect* and *reverence*, for those whose blood was shed so freely, to uphold the right, — please do not allude to it as "The Rebellion" nor as the no less reprehensible *"Civil War"* — but as the *"War* between the *States."*

The fortunes of war, have made us "conquered Provinces," a subjugated people, — with scarcely more resemblance, to the government of the Dominion of Canada, — but — *God rules*. He maketh the wrath of man, yea, even mans wickedness to work out *His* purposes.

But to the matter in hand, that of my reminscences, — When Virginia seceded, and the war commenced, I owned one young negro woman, for which, I had just three or four years previously, paid cash eleven hundred dollars in bank bills, worth their face value in gold, at any bank in the state, also one negro boy, a gift to my wife from her father. In the matter of stock, I had three work horses and one yearling colt, — (or rather filly) three or four cows, and some hogs. I owed some debts, and my credit unfortunately, was good for any reasonable amount. I continued, — as I had been doing before, to hire manual help on the farm, i.e. until every thing became completely unsettled, — the blockade broke up the exportation — and ultimately the cultivation of tobacco, — hence we had no money crop. Those of us at home subject to conscription, could make no arrangements for a years work. I was ordered before medical boards every few months, — ordered to "Camp Lee" camp of instruction three times before I was finally ordered to the army. This by way of explanation to show why and how it was, that my people were reduced to such a low state, in the matter of provisions when I did finally go into the army.

About the second year of the war, I sold the filly, which I had previously mentioned for $300 — she was afterward sold to a cavalryman for $1500. It becoming still more evident that I would ultimately have to enter the service, I sold another horse for $700. — When I finally entered the army, early in 1864 I left at home, perhaps as much as 2 barrels of corn, a part of a b*bl* of flour — with perhaps a month or two rations of meat, with some little rough feed, two horses, another young colt, afterwards sold at weaning time for $100 —) and 3 or 4 cows. Willy was then 5 or 6 years old, *Geo*

154

still younger, Lelia younger still, & Sallie just a few months old. About a month after I left home, some epidemic attacked the cows, — or some poisonous potion administered, & the last one died. By this time both bread & meat were just about used up, no milk, no anything for your mother, the children, & the negroes. By this time the government was impressing all the provisions it could lay its hands upon for the soldiers and their indigent families, hence it was hard to find either meat or bread, that could be purchased at *any price*. Your mother bought at exorbitant prices as long as it could be had, — by way of a smuggle. Vegetables had not yet come in, as it was still spring and early summer. At length, through the kind exertions of *Geo* Chambers and P.A. Forbes your mothers name was got upon the list of beneficiaries, drawing bread in very limited quantities from the government, no meat was issued. For coffee parched corn, wheat, rye & sweet potatoes were used.

Upon one occasion your mother got an order (from government) for 2½ bu of wheat, on Rbt Bolling (*Dr* Bolling's father). He lived down near Hardware. She had no one to send for it except *Geo* Luis, the negro boy, *scarcely*, if at all in his teens. He did not know the way, but he met up with Dr. Bolling who knew him, & kindly went with him down to his father's, saw him get the wheat and start for home while he remained awhile conversing with his father then came on by the same route Luis had to come. He hadn't made more than a mile or two before he came upon Luis, who had let his bag of wheat fall off the horse. He had led the horse up beside the bag, —got him two smooth fence nails, put one end of the rails up on the fleshy part of the horses rump, and was industriously, and heroically rolling the bag up, in fact had about got it up when *Dr* B. came up with him. On another occasion your mother had an order on a neighbor for some corn, she sent & got it, & before sending it to the mill, she had to spread it on a cloth & pick the rotten corn out of it, being evidently the sweepings of a corn crib run through a fan mill. Being entirely shut in by the blockade, many things we regarded as indispensable necessaries, was not to be had, among these none was more missed than *salt*. But our people by ingenuity, and indefatigable persistency managed to eke out the *very scant* supply. Our antebellum meat houses (or as they were called *smoke houses*) were built with dirt floors, — these dirt floors had been receiving the waste & drippings of salt for years & years, — this dirt was dug up by our people at home. Your mother among others, mixed with water, subjected to a boiling heat, which would throw to the surface, a scum or foam which taken off as it rose, and dropped into clean cold water, and the salt would settle to the bottom, leaving the impurities on the surface, to be drained off with the water. As a substitute for soda, clean nice corn cobs were taken, a large cast iron over-lid was turned upside down, on a bed of hot coals, the cobs put upon the concave side of the lid, — ignite them, and let the heat from the coals, continue & finish up the burning process. This would have a handfull of nice white ashes, which were cautiously and sparingly used as a substitute for soda.

While I was away, and before your mother had used up quite all of the little meat I left home, some rogue came one night and tried to break into the meat house by boring out enough of the weather boarding to make a hole large enough for entrance, but his auger was large, and split the boards, thus making a noise which attracted the attention of your mother, & of Vaden Ayres (Lucinda's husband) who happened to be here that night. Vaden came to the window & called your mother, & they went around the houses, but the thieves had absconded. At the second battle of Cold Harbor, I was wounded, & hospitals in Richmond being crowded I was sent to Petersburg. Of course I notified your mother as soon as I could, — using my left hand to write, my right being disabled. Your mother got W*m* A. Smith (who had a substitute in the army) — to take her to Farmville where they took the train for Petersburg. When they got there, I had gotten a furlough home, & not knowing how I could get home *Via* Farmville, I had gone Via Richmond, where I had to lie over a day and a night before I could get passage on the Packet Boat home. In the meanwhile, times were so critical around Petersburg & Richmond that your mother could not get passage to Richmond, so she had to return to Farmville. In the meanwhile when she took the train in Farmville, her horse & buggy had been sent 9 miles out from F. to the house of a relation, and so she, getting back earlier than she expected found herself without the means of transportation from Farmville, — but undismayed, she set out afoot, walked the 9 miles, got her horse and buggy & reached home the same day, a distance of 25 miles by buggy, after walking 9 miles. In the meanwhile before taking the Packet, I drew $60 commutation money, i.e. money for my board while out on the 60 day furlough. I paid *all* this for one l*b* of coffee in Richmond, and while on the boat paid $2.00 for one cup of coffee, without either milk or sugar. When I reached home, I found your mother there. This was about 15th June 1864. I found your Mother with 2½ bu. corn and perhaps 25 l*bs* flour, and not 10 l*bs* meat, and no corn at all, but with vegetables and fruits just beginning to come in, — neither bread nor meat could be bought except on the sly because all the surplus had been impressed (seized) by the government. As may be supposed, it did not take your mother, 4 children, myself, and two negroes very long to get through with the provisions on hand, — and how we managed to subsist, I cannot explain, nor can I myself, now understand. While at home I sold another horse and bought a cow at $600. Oh! how *proud* we were. The year 1864 was exceedingly dry, a disastrous crop year. Your M. did not gather as much as five l*bs* corn. That fall your M. had some 3 or 400 l*bs* meat butchered, fed almost entirely from the orchard which Mr Ayres owns now. In A*pl* 1865 I came home. Lee you know, surrendered on the 9*th* A*pl*. I found your M. & children with a few l*bs* of meat, a few meals of bread, not one dollar in currency — about $1000 left over of Confederate money — negroes freed, but with us — to be fed — as we could feed ourselves. I bought *on credit* one bbl of corn at $10.00 legal currency, vegetables just being planted, but we had our *COW!!* I went to work with one horse without feed. And of all the years I have seen, — the year 1865, was the most bounteous corn year. But how we lived until it grew is now almost inexplicable. After vegetables, potatoes, peas, and beans came in, with our butter and milk we fared *sumptuously*.

But you cannot tell how *bread* hungry we got along towards the fall. After finishing the cultivation of my corn crop — without feed, and not having good pasturage, — at your Grandfathers suggestion, I carried my horse down and put her in his pasture, and that is the last we have seen or heard of her. We suspect that she was killed & rolled into the river, by a negro, with whom I had had a difficulty.

About the time corn became glazed, — but still entirely too green to grind, — and feeling that we *must* have some bread, I took an old disused wash tin, and with a pegging awl, punched it full of holes, from the inside, so as to make the grate on the convex surface. — My grater being complete, I went to the field and gathered an armfull of corn, and set to work. The corn was so green it would choke my "mill" but we were too *bread* hungry to give it up, — and of all the dainty morsels I have eaten, I think *that* bread was the *sweetest*.

This grater was occasionally brought in requisition until the corn was in a condition to grind. That fall we gathered a bountiful crop of breadstuff & feed.

Thus far hath the Lord led us. And while our lot has at times, seemed very hard, yet when we look back, we can see much to be grateful for. Blessed be his Holy Name, — G. Hill Winfrey

∞

George Hill Winfrey, born 1835, died 1918; was married to Judith Catharine Robertson in 1856. She was born 1838, died 1915.

Chapter II.

War
Diaries
of Men
Who
Wore
the Gray

Through the courtesy of Miss Mary Ogg of Trevilians, Virginia, and the Louisa County Historical Society the most interesting letters and diary of Pvt. William W. Downer, Miss Ogg's grandfather, are presented here.

Private Downer was a resident of Orange Springs, Orange County, Va., and was a member of Company I, 6th Regiment, Virginia Cavalry, Lomax's Brigade, Fitz Lee's Division, Cavalry Corps, Army of Northern Virginia.

He was captured 13 August 1864 and imprisoned at the Federal Prisoners of War Camp at Camp Chase (Columbus) Ohio on 11 September 1864.

Letters and Diary of a Confederate Prisoner of War

William W. Downer
Private

Company I
6th Virginia Cavalry

Camp Chase Prison, Ohio
September 13th, 1864

Dear Lucie

The privilege of writing by flag of truce being allowed prisoners of war. I embrace this opportunity of writing you a few lines to inform you I am well and hope when this reaches you it may find you and the little children well. I shall write whenever an opportunity affords itself and I wish you to do the same. John Woolfolk or Doct Tom either will direct your letters for you. In writing confine yourself strictly to family affairs and not write more than half sheet of paper.

I was captured on the thirteenth of August and reached Camp Chase, Ohio on the fifth of September. I hope you will not take to heart our being sepperated for a time, and I also hope the day is not far distant when we shall meet again. Give my love to Ma and all the family, also to your Robert's family. Kiss my little children for me and tell them I hope to see them soon. You will direct your letter to Camp Chase Ohio Nothing more at present but remain your affectionate husband until death.

Wm. W. Downer

P.S.

Ferdinand Bearley and S.V. Corbell are prisoners with me. You can inform their friends where they are. We are all well.

Dec. 24th 1864

This is Christmas Eve and oh how lonely I feel. The thought of home and my dear wife and children being so far away from me and I confined in prison makes me feel as if

I had not a friend on earth, but, nevertheless I feel there is one who is able willing and ever ready to help us in time of need. In him I place my trust and ask for help and he alone. Oh that I could have enjoyed the presence and children as I expected on this particular occasion. Tonite as usual my little children will hang up their socks for old Chris to put something in for them; but they have no Pa Pa at home to fill them but; I hope their Ma Ma will fill them as we usually do. I feel like tonight my wife has offered up her prayer to God for my preservation and safe return to her and my little children. God grant that the time may speedily arrive when I shall be with my family again oh that I could say in the language of our Savior, not my will but thine be done. Oh God.

Dec. 25th 1864

Today is Christmas day and a most beautiful day it is. My thoughts are still on home. Last night I had a pleasant dream and felt truly happy until I was awakened and I realized nothing but a dream. I had been exchanged and reached home in safety. It was breakfast and my wife had prepared a large loaf of bread for breakfast. It was on the table smoking and a large pint of butter setting in the middle of the table. I was seated to the table and, oh; how I enjoyed it. I really thought the best I had ever eaten. My wife sitting at the head of the table looking upon me with delight not eating a mouthful.

Willie and Towles sitting on my left calling on Pa for something about every moment and my little baby sitting on the floor, when I was awakened, and, oh; what disappointment when I raised up in my bed and realized nothing more than a dream.

I thank God although I am sepperated from home and all that is near and dear to me I have health and strength. This morning I have a nice cup of coffee for breakfast given to me by Ferdinand Beasley being quite an addition to my breakfast. I am expecting to receive a box of clothes, tobacco and some money from cousin Tap Goodloe Baltimore City which will be a great relief to me. I hope it may come during the Christmas holiday. I have only received one letter from home as yet Dec. 25th 1864.

Dec. 26th 1864

Who shall separate us from the love of Christ—Romans 8th chapter, 35th verse. Nothing will! Nothing can! I may be seperated from friends, comrades, home all I must lose on earth, but those, oh blessed Redeemer, are always at my side. Even if death should overtake me it cannot sever from thee. Thine is a love, strong as death, surviving death, enduring as eternity. Surely he has borne our grief and carried our sorrows.—Isaiah 53rd Chapter, 4th verse. Am I now a great sufferer? What, after all, am I enduring? Only a few ripples in the tide of love whereas my Savior has borne and borne for me all the waves andbillows of wrath! Don't call prison with his, mine surely, are light afflictions.

Camp Chase Ohio   Jany 24th 1865
Prison #2 Barracks 15

Dear Lucie

I will again write you a few lines hoping they may reach you in safety. I have never received but one letter from you since I have been in prison and that was in October. I feel very anxious to hear from you and my little children. I hope it will not be long before we shall meet again. I thank God I am enjoying good health and have no right to grumble at my treatment as a prisoner. The confinement is all that I mind. Lucie write as soon as you receive this and give me the address of your sister in Kentucky and her name give me the address of Uncle Abner David. John Henderson in Missouri. James Henry Levill Aunt Ann Jackson and any other friend or relative that you or Ma or any other friend can think of. Ma can give you Aunt Ann Jackson's office. Also George Terrill Columbus Young. Do not fail to write immediately and give me the address of all that I mentioned. I am not in need of clothes. Cousin Tavener Goodloe has just sent me a full suit of clothes from Baltimore. I am in need of tobacco and money and could get it if I could get the offices of those I have mentioned. Kiss my little children for me and do not let them forget me. My love to you Lucie and Ma and all the children and tell them to write to me. My love to your brother Robert and family and tell them to write also. I hope this may find you and my little children well. I wish that I was allowed to write more but the rules of the prison will not allow more than one page and two letters a week. What a joyful time it will be with me when we meet again I think of you and my children so much from your devoted husband.

May God bless us and guide us through this life is my prayer.

Wm. W. Downer

167

February 5th 1865 Sunday morning

What a beautiful morning is this, and, what glorious news we have we have received this morning from Lieut. Sankey, Provost Marshall of prisoners. We are fully apprised of the fact this morning that a general exchange of prisoners is agreed upon and the rolls are now being made out for the purpose of transporting prisoners immediately. Oh, what joyful news to us who have not ceased praying to be returned to our homes and families night or day since our imprisonment. Blessed be the name of the Lord for he will deliver us in due time. I shall look forward to the time of my deliverance with much anxiety and pray to God for its speedy arrival. What happiness I must experience when I meet with my wife and children Mother Brothers and sisters and relations and friends. I know my wife will look with an anxious eye for my return and tell my little children that Pa will soon come home. God speed the time is my prayer, and will ever be.

Feb. 9th 1865

Today prisoners are being parolled preparatory to an exchange. The papers now inform us that a general exchange is certainly agreed upon. Some have been disposed to doubt it, although I have entertained fears upon the subject which is perfectly natural. Men confined in prison are hardly capable of judging rightly upon any subject from the fact they most always lean to the side that favors their cases mostly. We have suffered much since my imprisonment. My constant prayer to God has been to shield me from all dangers and difficulties and return me safely to my wife and children once more. I know my wife's anxiety at present expecting to hear of my arrival in Richmond every day.

Today is the 9th. I hope to leave Camp Chase by the 20th or 25th of the month. Should I be disappointed I shall try to bear it with fortitude. May the Lord give me health and courage to bear up under any and all misfortune.

Feb. 17th 1865

Today another batch of prisoners have left on exchange. Tis quite cheering indeed to see the men when ordered to pack up and be ready to fall into line for the roll to be called and then start off for their homes and friends in Dixie. How slowly time seems to pass of now, but perhaps I am too impatient my anxiety being so great to get home. I had hoped to get off by the 20th of February but I fear it will two or three long weeks yet before my departure from prison. May the Lord throw his all protecting arms around me and my little family and preserve us from all harm is the prayer of a poor humble sinner.

February 22nd 1865

Today my name has been called preparatory to an exchange. I am expecting everyday to be paroled be ready whenever called upon to start for home and friends in Dixie. Men are leaving very slowly now but I hope they will be moved more rapidly in a short time. The roads are used at present for transporting Federal troops to the front. We have a report that nine hundred will start in a day or two. I hope it is so. Two thousand has to leave before I can leave. The next chance will be mine.

March 2nd 1865

Today another squad of prisoners are being called to leave at 3 o'clock this evening. Lieut. Sankey Provost Marshall of prisons informed us another squad will leave saturday the 5th if so I expect by the blessing of God to leave next week. No one can imagine with what anxiety I look forward to the time of my departure from prison and more particularly to the time when I shall be able to meet my dear ones at home. Oh, what a joyful meeting it must be to embrace my wife and my little babes once more. My feelings can scarcely be suppressed. Tears come trickling down my cheeks, but, I feel not ashamed for sepparation from those we love so dearly is enough to melt the stoutest hearts. May God keep and provide for my dear wife and children, my aged and crippled mother my sisters and particularly my brothers who are exposed to the danger and turmoil of war. What a blessing to have God to look to when everything is dark and threatening around us. I thank God our Lord and savior Jesus Christ will make all bright around us in due time, for he has told us all things work together for our good.

March 4th 1865

Another squad of prisoners will leave this evening. This is the fifth batch of prisoners that has left on exchange. I fully expect with the help of God to get off next week in the sixth or seventh squad.

Oh how cheering to think the time of my departure from prison is next at hand. May the Lord bless and preserve us from all dangers and return me to my dear ones at home again. Oh Lord may my hopes of reaching home soon be realized. Teach me oh God, to put my trust in thee and thee alone.

March 19th 1865

This morning at two o'clock another squad of prisoners start on exchange. Oh, how I longed to go with them, but my time has not come yet. I confidently expect to start in the next lot of prisoners which will start between this and Wednesday next without something to prevent. Should have gone before now but for high water in James River. I wonder if my wife knows the reason why it is my coming home is so long delayed. I hope she does for I fear she has become very uneasy about me. May the Lord help her and comfort her and my little children. I thank God my time of departure is near at hand. Oh, how cheering it is to me to think my time for starting home is so near at hand and what glad tidings it would be to my wife and little ones if they only knew it. My prayer to Almighty God is that nothing may transpire to prevent me from going. Oh, what a happy time I must experience when at home once more with my dear wife and little ones. The suffering I have to undergo here I will not pretend to describe for it would take a quive of paper to describe it and then not be half told. With the help of God I will try and bear it with fortitude. Now may Almighty God take me and mine under his guidance and protection is my humble prayer.

Sunday 25th March 1865

Today a squad of sick and wounded leaves on exchange. We have a report that our squad will be detained to wait on them but I fear it is not true. Oh, what anxiety I have about leaving this place. I pray to God that I may get off as nurse today. We ought to have left some time ago but high waters prevented us from going and now the wounded and sick are thrown in before us. It seems hard but we must try and bear it with fortitude. I hope everything will turn out for the best. I feel more anxious on my wife's account than my own knowing or believing she does not know the reason why it is that my delay is so long. May God bless her and my little children and bring us to embrace each other before long is my prayer.

Henderson Co. Ky.
April 5 1865

Mr. Wm. W. Downer

Dear Sir

    I regret very much to say to you that I have just received your letter and hasten to answer uncertain whether you are still at Camp Chase as there has been so much said about "Exchange of Prisoners" of late I send you some tobacco and if you will write immediately and let me know if you are still in Prison I will do what I can for you. I will now state why I did not get your letter sooner. About the time your letter was written I was qualified assessor of Henderson Co. Ky. and my duties called me from home the Ohio River got out of its banks and I was not able to come home for a month consequently your letter dated March 1st did not reach me until April 4th so you must think it was neglect on my part when you write let me know who of my acquaintances are prisoners of war. Where is Jack Sale. Anything you can tell me of my old friends & school mates will be edifying where are all of the boys from around Orange Springs Write soon

Your old friend
John T. Moon
Direct to   Henderson P.O.   Ky.

May 31st 1865

I had heretofore concluded to stop writing, fearing my mind was centered too much upon worldly pleasures and things at home. Not looking to God as our helper in time of need that being the only source by which we can drive any real blessings or benefits. I have tried to pray earnestly to our Lord and Savior Jesus Christ for pardon of all my sins, for my deliverance from prison, and my return to my family, to take care of my family in my absence and guide and direct my wife what is best to do in all cases. I know not how to pray as I ought, may the Lord teach me how to pray and to live a better mass the remainder of my days.

I have no doubt that my long imprisonment is for some good and just cause, but oh, how hard for such poor frail creatures as we are to be convinced of it. God grant that the time may speedily come when I shall enjoy the privileges of being with those loved ones at home again.

Since receiving my wife's last letter I have felt somewhat depressed in spirits, as someone has been so unkind as to tell her I could return home if I felt disposed but would not come.

Inconstancy to my wife and children; God forbid. He who knoweth all things knoweth my heart that such a thought or such a feeling never, no never entered this heart of mine. Oh, that my wife could know my feelings since receiving her letter, and I know her heart would sympathize with mine. But why write thus, to wound her feelings? No, never, but, only to express my own.

The presidents proclamation having been issued yesterday we are all expecting to hear something respecting our release everyday. May the Lord bless us all and soon unite me with my family again is my prayer.

I have this morning read my wife's letter again and in spite of my efforts to suppress them, tears came trickling down my cheeks to think someone I know not who, has been so unkind to tell my wife that I could come to her assistance but would not. This is the way of the world instead of trying to console her while we are imprisoned someone is trying to get up disension and strife. Will the Lord help her to look upon me as she did I believe before our seperation; not as one ready to desert her in these dark hours of trial but, on a loving husband ready and willing at all times to aid and assist her under any and all circumstances. May God bless my wife and little children. Help my wife, Oh, God to exert a proper influence my little boy and train them up in the way they should go. I know she needs a father to help her train them up and I hope the time is not far distant when we shall be together again. What anxiety I suffered no one knows. We are told that the authorities are hourly expecting orders for our release and have been for several days. The time is long but we must bear it as becometh Christians.

Prisoner of War
Camp Chase Ohio
June 5th 1865

Dear Mother
I send you my prison books to read if you wish. Take care of them and when you are done with them return them as I wish to keep them as long as I live.

Having written to my wife on our last mail day I am anxious to know if there is any probability of her receiving my letters. The one I received has no post mark is to her than Fortress Monroe. What is the cause of this I know not. I should have written regularly hertofore but was informed and expecting to start home every day I would not venture to write hoping to reach home and take them all by surprise. My wife in writing often tells me what Touck says he must tell me about coming home, but if I recollect right has never mentioned Willie more than once in that respect. It is possible my little boy has forgotten me as not to ask his Ma anything about me and when his Pa is coming home. I hope not perhaps for being at school and away from his Ma Trough the day his mind is not brought to bear so much upon his Pa.

And there is my little baby his Ma, Ma says a sweet little fellow that does not know that he has a Pa except from what he has been taught by his fond mother. To think that I have a child now twelve months old and not even know his name. I wrote to his Ma last winter but do not know that she received the letter telling her what I desired his name should be as she requested me in one of her letters. And is this all I have to trouble me, not by a great deal. At my far home is a widowed and crippled mother dependent on her sons for support. One of which I fear from late intelligence received from home cannot survive long owing to a wound received in the campaign of 1864. And the Mrs. son wounded through the arm and still away from home. I am though I hope not confined in prison. And this is not at all yet, there are five sisters four of whom are single and no one to look to for help except their brothers. After all there is one consolation they have an education sufficient to make them a good living. We should thank God for this for it is a great blessing. Though left in a needy condition yet we can look around us and see hundreds in a great deal worse condition than they are. Let us not raise a voice of complaint against

the cause of my staying away from those I love so well, and someone has been so unkind as to tell her it was my fault that I did not come to them. God only knows my heart, and when I reach home and reveal to her those truths. I know it will be hurtful to her feelings to think that she has for a moment harboured the thought within her breast that I could for a moment be untrue to her or those little ones I have left behind me. I fear in theirs I may cast a gloom over my wife's feelings, but if so I hope she will pardon me for it.

I know she knows and feels it is not my wish ever to cast the least shade upon her feelings, for of all these are some that I love so tenderly as her. As it is now nearly dark I shall have to stop writing. May the Lord watch over us; and guide and direct us in all his ways; and when done with us here on earth save us at last in his kingdom above is the prayer of this sinful heart of mine.

June 10th 1865

I have been waiting and mostly all this evening at the gate of the prison hoping to be called out to take the oath and start for home. Today being Saturday I shall not be able to get off now before Monday; when I hope if the Lord is willing to be able to start for home to meet those dear ones I long to see so much. The nearer the time approaches the more anxious and restless I am. To sit in silent repose and think of those dear ones at home that I so soon hope to meet what a thrill of joy passes over this heart of mine. The lonely and miserable hours that I have spent in prison, I hope, has learned me a lesson that I shall never forget. I must acknowledge my thoughts have been too much on the things of this world, and too little upon our Lord and Savior Jesus Christ, from whom and by whom we receive very good and precious gift. Though I have suffered a great deal since my imprisonment with cold and hunger; even to be so much reduced as to be hardly able to walk across the enclosure of the prison, yet; there has been times even in my gloomiest hours that I could look to my God with a prayerful heart and receive that reconciliation that none but the Lord can give. I have never for a moment since my imprisonment believed otherwise than that by the grace of God I should be returned to my family again. I have seen men of every age and every description langushing in prison with their minds riveted upon home and suffer their minds so to run until disease would soon overtake them and they would be no more. Life how uncertain, death how certain.

Many a man since my imprisonment apparently in good health has been stricken down without the shortest notice, even while prominading the streets or partaking of scanty means, But few middle aged men and old men have survived. No one knows who has not witnessed it; the feelings that must necessarily arise when we see from day to day from thirty to fifty of our comrades taken to their last resting place, for us never more to behold their faces until that awful trumpet shall sound and one and all of us shall have to obey its calling. Many have died happy and many have died without one ray of hope.

It is distressing indeed to visit the hospital and see these men with their lips parched with burning fever begging for water and for help and everything their poor appetites might erase; and in many instances taking the name of the Lord their God in vain as if their salvation depended upon such conduct. There are many things about which I might write but for want of time and space.

Sunday morning June 11th 1865

I am informed releasing will be kept up all day in order that the men may take the early trains from Columbus tomorrow morning; there being no trains on Sunday. What a beautiful morning, the sun has just risen with all its beauty and splendor and everything bids fair to have a beautiful day. I hope to leave Camp Chase today and spend the night at Columbus for the purpose of taking the six o'clock train tomorrow morning. May the Lord in all his mercy take charge of one and all of us guiding and directing us in the way we should walk.

Monday June 12th 1865

Having obtained my release yesterday evening I immediately left Camp Chase for Columbus. I reached this place yesterday evening but being Sunday I could not obtain transportation until this morning. I now have all things ready to leave for home on the 2 o'clock train this evening. I can hardly realize that I am once more free from prison. I hope soon if it be the will of God to embrace those dear ones at home that have wept and mourned so long for my coming. I thank thee Oh, Lord for those that delivered me out of prison. What a blessing it is that we have a crucified redeemer to look to, who is always our best and surest support; let the storms go their around us as dark as they may. With the Lord for our support we have nothing to fear, not even death itself. May the Lord watch over and protect me and my family from all harm and soon return me to them is my humble prayer.

June 13th 1865

At Bellaire last night 10 o'clock. Walked up to Wheeling this morning and had to wait for transportation until 4 o'clock this evening. We expect to take the train tonight at ten o'clock. I am now about to draw rations and repair to the depot.

June 14th 1865

Owing to discharged northern soldiers being transported to their homes we were compelled to lay over at Wheeling until 4 o'clock this morning when we left for Baltimore.

June 15th 1865

We are still on the road in open flat cars and raining hard. We are all quite wet but willing to undergo anything to get home.

June 16th 1865

Arrived at Baltimore 10 o'clock in the morning and went directly to the Quartermasters office for transportation. Had a good deal of sympathy and kindness shown us while in the city. Left Baltimore for Fortress Monroe 6 o'clock in the evening of the 16th. Arrived at Ft. Monroe about 12 o'clock the 17th. Went into camp about two miles from wharf and drew rations. We expect to leave for Richmond tomorrow morning.

I have just been into the bay and taken a good wash. I feel much better since washing for I was blacker and dirtier than I ever was in my life. I had hopes to reach home this evening, but we have been so much detained on account of transportation I have no hopes of reaching home before Monday next unless we get to Richmond sooner than I expect. We are camped among the Yankees and the boys are mingling about among them generally selling rings, breast pieces and many other tricks made while in prison.

June 18, 1865 Sunday morning

We are now at the Quarter Masters Office awaiting our tickets for transportation. Everything works quietly and no disrespect shown us. The Yankee soldiers tell us boys you all fought well but we were too strong for you. I tell them not until our men deserted their cause and went over to them, which they acknowledge. Reached City Point half past three o'clock in the evening; landed the southern troops at that point and left for Richmond at 4 o'clock. Expect to reach Richmond by dark. Reached Richmond at dark and went to the Capital square and stayed all night.

June 19th 1865

I am now on board the train and hope to reach home this evening. What a joyful time for us all to meet again. May the Lord keep us safely and return us to our families soon.

The following was written on the last page of the diary:

My wife's address
Mrs. Lucie M. Downer
Orange Springs
Orange County, Va.

My wife's address was written down in this book in the event of my death that some one would be kind enough to inform her of it.

The diary, written on lined note paper 3 5/8" by 5 1/2" held together by two pieces of very thin string, along with the letters, are on display in the Louisa County Historical Society Museum, Louisa, Virginia.

William W. Downer

Confederate Dead Remembered
Camp Chase Cemetery

There remains today at the site of the old Camp Chase Military Prison a Confederate Cemetery established in 1863, the largest north of the Mason-Dixon Line. The cemetery is located on a two acre plot on the west side of Columbus, Ohio, where 2,260 loyal men in gray died while prisoners of war.

Each year, on Confederate Memorial Day, the Dixie Chapter, United Daughters of the Confederacy of Columbus, Ohio, conducts a memorial service for these remembered veterans of the Lost Cause.

Members of the Sons of Confederate Veterans 22nd Virginia Infantry and Sons of Union Veterans 1st Ohio Infantry fire a salute honoring these Southern soldiers.

Shown below is a newspaper account of the ceremony held at the cemetery on June 2, 1974, at which the author may be seen in the left center of the picture. The other picture shows the Memorial Arch of rough hewn granite blocks which was erected and unveiled on June 7, 1902.

Dead Soldiers Honored—*Memorial Services were attended by more than 100 persons Sunday at Camp Chase Cemetery honoring the 2,240 Confederate prisoners of war buried there, Robert H. Carlile, assistant vice president of the Huntington National Bank, was the speaker.* (Photos by C-J Photographer Herb Workman)

183

Confederate Cemetery and Monument, Camp Chase, Ohio

B

Diary
of
Private
Benjamin
Haggason
Sims

Bertram I. Allen of Louisa, Va., has provided the diary of Private Benjamin Haggason Sims, his grandfather, who lived on a farm at Alto Post Office several miles north of Louisa, in Louisa County, Virginia.

Lucian and Robert, referred to in the diary, were his brothers.

He was a member of Co. I, 17th Va. Infantry, also known as the O'Connell Guards, Alexandria, Va., which was commanded by Captain Raymond Fairfax. The unit was a part of Corse's Brigade, Longstreet's Corps, Army of Northern Virginia.

He is buried in the family cemetery on a farm several miles north of Louisa on Route 669 which is owned by C.M. Winston.

Diary of
Benjamin Haggason Sims

I Benja. H. Sims left home near Alto P.O. in Louisa County, Virginia Sunday morning Sept. 13th. 1863. A very pretty day over head but a little muddy underfoot. Riding our little mule Jerry, he is about 4 feet 6 or 8 inches high. In the first place I take the mail bags over to the contractor T.N. Smith here I find out that Jas McGraw a young fellow of my acquaintance about my age has gone on to Salem, a church about 8 miles distant where we have previously agreed to be together, so I set out to overtake which I do in about 1½ miles. We then go on to church together and get there before the congregation begins to collect. So we go over to a house near by where Jim is acquainted with some ladies. Here we stay until church-time when we walk with the ladies to church. We then stand about the yard until up comes Miss S.A. Hill. I go at once to the carriage where I talk with Miss H. awhile before going in church. We then have a very good sermon by Mr. McChesney. I then take dinner with Miss H. and at her request stay to hear the evening sermon. I then bid her farewell and set out for an old bachelors relation's "who is one in every sense of the term" to stay all night. I find him quite unwell, but he tells me a great many funny tales as usual. Monday morning I set out for the C.H. nine miles distant which I make in very good time. Here I try to find the enrolling officer to get a pass to go and join the comp. my brother Lucian is in, stationed 6 miles above Gordonsville but fail to find him so I conclude to go ahead and risk chances but when I get in 4 miles of Gordonsville I meet with a squad of Capt. Andersons detective guards who say I must go with them. Well I think to myself if I must I must. So on I go with them to catch some deserters. We have a shower of rain and get wet but get one deserter. We then go on to Gordonsville where I am carried before Major Boyle who says I am a conscript and sends me to the guard house about sunset Monday evening. Here my feelings are very much cut and don't sleep any worth speaking of that night. Next day Mrs. Phillips an acquaintance of mine sends over some eatables to me. My feelings are so much hurt I feel very little like talking. Wednesday morning I feel somewhat relieved by being sent to Orange C.H. where I stay in Capt. A's room until Thursday when I, with one H.H. Mills of Warren Co. are sent to Richmond. About sunset we get to R. and set out for Camp Lee where we get about dark. Here I feel entirely relieved that is I pass it all off. Mr. M. and myself go into Sergt. Williams mess. Here I get some clothing, eatables etc. from home. After a time Mr. M. is sent to the Co. he selects. As the weather begins to get cool we move in the barracks. I go up stairs with the Sergt. where I fare very well. Here I write to Miss H. for the first time just a short note written with a pencil. But before I get an answer we are sent to Ivor Station. I with some 45 or 50 others were called up Oct. 22nd. and told that we were going to be sent to another camp of instruction and that we would be allowed the privilige of selecting our comp. there as well as at Camp Lee. We arrived at Petersburg in the night of the 22nd., the train having been delayed on the way, a distance of 22 miles. Here we staid all night. Next morning we set out for Ivor Station 36 miles east of Petersburg. We arrived at Ivor Station about noon on the 23rd. Oct. Here the most of us were decently taken in. We were just put in the 17th. Regt. Va. Infty. with no chance for a transfer. Some of us wore pretty long faces but it gradually wore off until most of us were as well satisfied, I have no doubt, as if we had been sent to the companys we wished. At Ivor we had very comfortable quarters. We went twice on raids down in Isle of Wight Bay but had no fighting to do. On the first raid we were allowed to have no fire and consequently suffered very much with cold. Shortly after our arrival at Ivor I rec. an answer from

Miss H. and from that we took up regular correspondence. Nothing of very great importance occured while at Ivor. We left Ivor Jan'y 23rd. about the same time in the day that we got there just 3 months previous and came up to Petersburg where we arrived a little after night. We staid in Camp near Petersburg until Jan'y 28th. when we take the train for N. Carolina and come to Weldon where we stay all night. Next day we go on to Goldsboro and from thence to Kinston where we arrive in the night. Here we stay until about 12 o'clock next day and set out on the march for Newbern a distance of some 59 miles which we made in 40 hours over the sandiest road I ever saw. I never saw more sore feet and broken down men before. We arrived at our position near Newbern Monday morning Feb'y 1st '64 where we staid in line of battle until noon Wednesday. We were pretty close to the enemy and could hear their guns and the band playing dixie. During the night we could see the light from their Arty fire etc. On Wednesday we started back and as it happened were not molested but we expected to be. Most of us crossed a creek some 15 feet deep on planks not more than a foot wide. Thursday evening we got back to Kinston where we staid all night and then set out on the march for Goldsboro 29 miles which we made by Sunday evening. Here we staid until Feb. 24th. When we got marching orders about dark we then went to the depot at Goldsboro and drew rations and about nine o'clock P.M. we took the train for Lexington but we didn't know where we were going until we got there. At Lexington we found quite a pretty country, red & rolling with plenty of oak and hickory and the people the kindest I have seen since I left home. They fairly feasted us and at the same time thought it was casting insinnuations on them for us to be sent up there. But we just had a grand time sitting back in the C.H. with cain bottom chairs and carpeted floor and walk out to see the ladies any time as we had no guard duty and no drills. But we were soon cut short in this fun. On the 5th March we got orders to go back to Goldsboro where we staid until the 7th. when we went to Kinston where we take up camp about two miles from town. Our rations are pretty good here. The country all in this section is flat and sandy with plenty of swamps and pines. March 21st cloudy and some round snow and cold rain. 22nd. cold with snow hail or rain all day. 23rd. ground covered with snow and we have a snow balling with Hokes N.C. Brig. the above was written March 24th.'64. March 29th. cloudy and we have a tremendous rain storm in the evening and a good many of the tents get flooded but ours happens to be better than some others. After the storm the sun comes out and I get 2 letters which have been due a good while. April 1st. we and three Regts. of the Brig. present are carried out to witness the execution of a member of Co. G of the 17th. Regt for desertion. He was shot to death with musketry and the first man I ever saw killed. In the evening we have rain. Apr. 2nd. rainy but clears off in the evening and we have dress parade when our comp. I is complimented by Gen'l Corse for the good order in which our guns are kept. But after parade is over we are sent to the ordnance wagons to get other guns which we find to be a very rough and ugly gun, but a much lighter bayonet than those we turn over. Apr. 10th. we leave camp about 2 o'clock P.M. and start on the march for Newbern. Take up camp about sundown. Sleep tolerably well. Start next morning about 7 o'clock and march till about 4½ o'clock P.M. When we meet the Yankee Picketts and turn back. We come back about 4 miles and take up camp again for the night. Get up pretty soon next morning and set out for camp where we arrive about 2 o'clock P.M. When the mail comes we get the first number of a paper we had subscribed for dated 12th. April '64. Apr. 30th. we have a general review of the forces at and near Kinston. General Corse and Walker are present. After we return to camp we are mustered in for pay. May 3rd. start for the 3rd time to

Newbern and a different road each time. About 12 o'clock on the 5th. we come to the Yankee outpost. They fire one shot and run. We then advance and take our position east of town where we are shelled pretty thick and heavy. Sleep tolerably well that night and start on the retreat about 12 M. on the 6th. Have a pretty hot and dusty march back and arrive at camp Sunday the 8th. Monday evening we go to Kinston to take the train for Va. but don't get off until 12 M. Tuesday. We are delayed on the way for a want of water and we get in 30 miles of Petersburg where the R.R. has been burnt and go in camp for further orders. Next morning we march 8 miles where some bridges have been burnt and it rains all the way very hard, some of the time. We then take the train again for Petersburg where we arrive about midday and find the city full of rumors about the Yankees between there and Richmond. In the evening we start on the march for R. go 4 miles and stay all night. We are quite wet all night. Next morning we are ordered back to take the S.S.R.R. immediately to meet raiders going towards the high bridge. We go up to the junction with the R. & D.R.R. and go down past Amelia C.H. to flat creek bridge. Here we meet the raiders and take our position behind a rock dike. Next morning they attack us very soon. The 14th. we fight them 2½ hours. When they leave we lose 3 men killed and one slightly wounded. The enemy lose 18 killed and some very badly wounded. It is reported they carry off their slightly wounded. On the 15th. we start for R. and go about 5 miles raining hard nearly all the way. When we stop at a burnt station and hear that the Yankees are coming back to burn the bridge. We get on a train of cars we have met and go back to the bridge and stay an hour or two when we get orders to go at once to R. where we arrive about midnight and get orders to sleep on the train till morning. In about an hour we get orders to take the R. & P.R.R. and go down near Drurys Bluff where we arrive about daybreak on the 16th.

and just at this time the ball opens for general engagement. We get off the cars and march round about 2 miles and take our position behind a bluff. The heaviest kind of musket firing was going on all the time. We soon get orders to advance to our breast works. We take our position behind the works and in two or three hours we charge the enemy and drive them from their rifle pits. We charge them about a mile and then advance a mile or two and stay all night. 17th. we advance about 4 miles from line of battle. About 9 P.M. we commence entrenching and have some heavy picket firing. 3 o'clock A.M. the 18th. our comp. is sent out on picket. We have heavy picket firing all day and dig rifle pits twice. We are relieved after dark and return to our line of works. About dark on the 19th. our Brig. is ordered to Richmond. We march till about midnight and take up camp for the night. On the morning of the 20th. we march into R. stay on the capital square until 21st when we take the train R & H pretty soon and go out to pole-cat station. At P.Cat the enemy are reported very near us. We go about a mile from the station and stay all night. Next morning we move on back via Mt. Carmel church to the Junction. Ewells and Longstreets corps ahead of us. Night of the 22nd I visit Lucian and Robt. who are camped about a mile and a half from us. 23rd. we move camp about a mile and stay until about dark when we move out and go 3 or 4 miles up the Central R.R. where we form lines of battle in a very flat and swampy place and throw up b. works. 25th. the enemy throw some 8 or 10 shells and we have some rain. 26th. more rain. 27th. we are roused about 2 hours before day with orders to move at once but we don't move until 8 o'clock when we go towards Richmond passing near the Hanover Academy and Ashland. Then we bear to the left and go towards the Mechanicksville turnpike. Take up camp before we get to the pike and spend a very quiet day Sunday the 29th. 30th. in the evening we move down to our line of breast works and get a position late at night. After night on 31st. we move farther to the right. June 1st. we move on to the right about a mile and throw up earth works. June 2nd. I with 3 others of my Co. go on picket with Co. D. At 7 P.M. on the 3rd. we are driven in but the enemy don't advance so we go back. For the last two days there has been heavy fighting on both wings or flanks. June 11th. our company was on picket yesterday. Nothing but picket firing since we were on before and in our front the enemy brought up a pretty heavy force to our front last evening. We have been expecting an attack but it hasn't come on yet. June 13th. the enemy left our front last night. About 8 o'clock A.M. we start for Malvern Hill about 15 miles and pass Gaines farm and the old battlefield of 7 pines. We bivouac about a mile from the Hill at Sunset, and stay all night June 14th. We exchange our guns again the Austrian rifle for the Enfield. June 16th. we start about sunrise for Petersburg via Drury's Bluff. After a very hard march we meet the enemy in ambush near Chester Station. We form line and drive them back till we occupy our line of works that we threw up about a month ago. After night we move on to a line of works that have been thrown up in advance of our old line which we find to be a very formidable line of works. 17th. our Regt. is on picket in front of these works. 18th. we move about a mile to the right. 19th. our Co. is on picket again, 20th. we move back to the place we first occupied on the left and just as we get back one of our Co. accidently shoots himself. 21st. all quiet till about 12 M. when the enemy gunboats and a heavy battery of ours commence shelling each other slowly and continue till night when everything becomes very quiet. 22nd. All very quiet. This is known as our position near Bermuda Hundreds. 23rd. All quiet till about night we shell the enemy's picket line. 24th. We are on picket and have a quiet day of picketing. 25th. All quiet and the weather is very hot and dry. 26th. All quiet and very hot. In the evening we have a slight shower but it don't cool the air much. 27th. All quiet and gets pretty cool at night from a cloud that passed round. 28th. Quiet. 29th. we are on picket all quiet. 30th. Quiet. July 1st 2nd 3rd Quiet. 4th. on picket very quiet. 5th 6th 7th & 8th quiet. 9th. on picket quiet. 10th. 11th 12th & 13th quiet. 14th. on picket, quiet. 15th 16th 17th 18th, quiet. 19th. on picket quiet and rainy all day. We got wet. This is the first rain we have had to lay the dust since about the first of June. 20th 21st 22nd 23rd. quiet. 24th. our company is on picket but I don't go out as I am sick and have been since we were on before. Night of 24th it rains nearly all night. 25th 26th 27th 28th quiet. 29th. our company on picket. I am still sick. 30th 31st Aug. 1st quiet. 2nd most of our Co. on picket. 8th. I resume duty by going on picket. All quiet since the 2nd. . . . . on the picket line. Our pickets advanced on the enemys pickets but we did not gain anything and lost several wounded. We had a rain about a week ago that refreshed things generally. Sept. 24th. we were startled this morning at 9 A.M. by the enemy's opening on our whole line with both field and mortar pieces, but it all turned out to be a salute. Nothing of importance since my last date. Our rations have changed from bad bacon and corn bread to beef and flour. Oct 21st we have another salute from the enemy. Nov. 18th. nothing of interest since my last date till last night the two Brigades on our right charge and capture the enemy's picket line taking some 120 prisoners with quite a small loss. 19th. we had some heavy picket firing last night and shelling today on the right. Dec. 29th. We are presented with an elegant dinner by the citizens in the neighborhood of flat creek bridge R. & D.R.R., Amelia County in token of a fight we had with some raiders at the bridge. Jan'y 4th. 1865 we leave camp about 8 P.M. and come about 8 miles over here to Fort Gilmer, ground covered with snow. We have tents to go into but we don't like the position at all. Sunday Feb'y 12th. The wind is such that it might be called a hurricane or storm all day and very cold. There are few clouds. A good many tents blew down. All are more or less racked. Our rations for the last 3 days and the next 3 have only been bread with sugar & coffee instead of meat. Feb'y 24th we start for our old position in front of Bermuda 100's at 11 o'clock P.M. where we arrive at day light after a very dark and muddy march. Mar. 5th. we start quite soon and go about a mile to the rear and remain in an old field till nearly night. We move into the woods and bivouac for the night. Mar. 7th. we go over to Picketts Head Qrts. where the Div. is reviewed. We come back and on the 8th we move across the pike and take up camp. 9th. we start after dark and have quite a muddy march through and about 2 miles above Richmond where we occupy a line of breast works to keep back a heavy body of raiders. On this move the moon shown in her full glory. We came out on the Brook pike and then followed the works round until we got below the nine mile road and bivouac for the night. 13th. we move back about 2 miles to the left. 14th. we move on back to the Brook pike, go up it 5 or 6 miles and turn towards Hanover Junction. We get to a place we camped at last summer when on our way to Cold Harbor. 15th. we move on up the Telegraph road to Ashland where we have a little skirmish with the enemy. After night we go about 5 miles towards Hanover C.H. 16th. we move on till we cross the Central R.R. at Peakes Sta. we then go in camp. 17th. I am on detail to go back to Peakes and help unload pontoons. They don't come till nearly night when we set out to join the Regt. about 4 miles off which we do a little after dark. 18th. We march 15 miles via Mechanicsville inside the Richmond fortifications and camp for the night. 19th. We start at day break and go down to our outer works about 2½ miles. 20th. We move in the woods to the rear and take up camp. 21st. We go up near Richmond where the Div. is reviewed again. It rains and we get wet before we get back to camp. 25th. We start before

2 o'clock A.M. and go up to Richmond to take the train for Petersburg but just before the train is ready to leave the order is countermanded and we come back to camp. 26th. we start before 1 A.M. and go up to Richmond and take the train for Petersburg. We got off 2 miles before we got to town and go out in the woods and take up camp. 29th. we go to the S.S.R.R. and take the train and go about 10 miles, get off and go about a mile and take up camp. 30th. we start about 2 o'clock A.M. and go out to the right of our lines where we form line of battle. It was raining hard all the time. In the evening we move on to the right and stay all night, still raining. 31st we move on down towards Dinwiddie C.H. where we have a fight and drive the enemy a mile or two. Our loss is pretty heavy. Apr. 1st. we fall back to the right of our lines, form line of battle and fix up temporary works. The enemy out flank us about night and 3 or 4 divisions of our army are completely stampeded, and we take to the woods, every man for himself. I got with 2 of my Comp. about a mile from the field. We stay all night together. On the 2nd we go on to the Appomattox River where I get with my messmate Old. We can't cross the river so we go on with the Regt. up the river to another crossing marching on after night. Old and I get missed of the Regt. and then conclude to go home. 3rd. we push on up to the R. & D.R.R. Bridge where we cross and go on up towards Powhatan C.H. We stay all night in a barn. 4th We go by P.C.H. and from thence to Cartersville on Jas. River where we intend to cross but can't. So we decide to go on to Lynchburg. We go about a mile from town and stay all night. 5th. we go on by Waltons Mill where we get some coarse flour and meet with an old lady who will have us go by with her and get dinner. She gave us as much bread as we could carry. We then go on to within 10 miles of Buckingham C.H. and stay all night. 6th. we pass the C.H. leaving it to the right some 4 or 5 miles and go on by Appomattox C.H. when we camp for

the night. 7th. we go on to Lynchburg where we cross the river and go out to Old's fathers where we arrive about midnight. I remain at Mr. Olds where I am very kindly treated until the 10th. when I set out for home. I get within one mile of Tye River where I stay all night with one Mr. Richardson, with whom I met during the day and we decided to make our journey together. 11th. we go on till we get 7 miles past Rockfish river on the Orange R.R. as we have decided to travel the R.R. when we stop with Dr. Brown. 12th. We continue our march by Charlottesville and stop for the night at Col. Randolph's. 13th. we go on by Gordonsville and stay all night with Mr. Joe Phillips. 14th. we come on by Louisa C.H. and stay all night at Uncle Seldon Sims. 15th. We get home about 2 o'clock P.M. weather wet and cloudy.

Benjamin Haggason Sims